WHITETAILS IN THE WIND

The Untold Secrets of Trophy Bow Hunting

By

Robert Fassbinder

Whitetails in the Wind

Publisher: Robert Fassbinder

ISBN 979-8-9948972-0-1

To: Kathy, Anne, Ben, Carol, and Mathew

Whitetails in the Wind

Table of Contents

Introduction

Whitetails in the Wind

Introduction

In the last fifty years bow hunting has undergone many changes. Some older hunters might argue that we were better off when we would go days without seeing a deer but never cross the path of another hunter. Today the whitetail draws ten times the number of hunters as it did back in 1970. The deer are more wary but there are more of them. Changes in the land use by agriculture, food plots by hunters, changes in forestry, DNR hunting season adjustments, hunting equipment, media hype, and on and on have all made the whitetail the focus of many more people. But still, when done well, bow hunting is without a doubt one of the most powerful experiences a human being can be given, connecting one to the beauty of this world which escapes so many. Just a close encounter with a mature whitetail buck can be a memory treasured forever. That is why I have written this book, to share with others a better way to get it done.

Chapter 1: The Learning Curve

"The Roots of Education are Bitter, but the Fruits are Sweet"
Aristotle

It was not until October 1981, ten years into bow hunting without a trophy deer to show for it, that I found myself in a huge burr oak at the top of a long, steep, wooded ridge. The very top of the ridge was a field of freshly picked corn with more timber on the far side. Balancing on a couple of limbs with my back against the trunk at 4 o'clock in the afternoon, I was about to begin learning a fundamental lesson for a still novice bow hunter. Across the field from the cover on the other side came a heavy nine point straight at me. I did not know that at the base of my tree was a spring flowing right out of the hillside. He was thirsty and I was rattled. He put his head down right under me. My first shot peeled the hair off his far shoulder. He leaped back ten yards and stood for what seemed like forever. Not knowing what that was all about, he cautiously came back for another drink. This time I did it right.

After the season I came back to that spot. Remembering the wind direction, I proceeded across the field to the cover on the far side from where he had come.   There it was, a very thick chunk of cover elevated slightly above everything around it.   With the right wind, he could smell everything behind him and see everything in front. It was not until years later that I figured out why he left that secure place to walk WITH THE WIND for a drink of water. There were several reasons. It was 1981 and early in the season, which meant less pressure. He was walking into an open field where he could see in all directions. He did not see me crawling into the big oak just inside the timber edge.   And last, I just got plain lucky.

After discovering this I thought, "Wow, it will be easy from now on." But as those of you with years of bow hunting behind you know, that is not exactly how it is.   I soon learned that you don't hunt the big guys in their own bedroom. But they do like to visit the ladies' bedrooms and they will be bedded in daylight.

The very next year in the very same area on the second to the last day of the November season, I finished up my morning watch in a snowstorm. Heading back to the truck, I spotted a large track right on the road. It was big enough to get anyone's attention. Rather than trying to track him to his bed (having failed at that many times) I decided to see where he had been. After taking the tracks through two nice beds, I spooked a real nice eight point with a real reddish coat. Continuing on the trail through two more beds, I found what looked like the perfect setup. The fact that where I considered the beds to be had no does did not bother me. The fact that he had visited them was reassuring. I was convinced that this was not a buck wandering aimlessly. He was hunting!

I checked out the downwind side of the bed, and hoping the wind would hold through the night, I picked a climbable tree and decided to check it out. Pulling the bow up, I decided I could stay for a half an hour. Less than fifteen minutes had passed when I spotted the buck I had spooked earlier coming to the bed. He marched right into the downwind side and gave me a perfect quartering away shot. This experience convinced me that beds could be hunted successfully. Recognizing them is not hard once you realize what the does need to be comfortable. They want to use their nose, their eyes, and their ears to keep them safe. The best use of their eyes is from an elevated position. Their nose needs to be downwind of the area behind them as well as picking up the thermals from the slope in front. However, their ears will work only in the quiet. A wind greater than ten miles per hour seems to make them very uneasy, and will have them burrowing low under thicker cover than they are usually comfortable with. A doe's bed will not have the extremely heavy cover of a mature buck. But during the rut, a buck will spend time in doe beds waiting for one to come along.

After the season, I continued to look for beds and the perfect tree to stand in. The snow made it easy to see which beds were frequented the most. I even wrote up a catalog with beds for each wind direction. In the years to come, I kept a log of how many deer came into the bed I was watching that day. Soon I didn't need any more convincing. In my mind this was it.

There were however some limitations with this new found method. Beds did not seem to work well for evening hunts. By late afternoon the deer were heading out for food or rut. Besides, you ran the risk of spooking them if you approached their bed in daylight. Nor would they work in high winds. But probably the most difficult thing to address was that a given bed would only work for one wind direction plus or minus 30 degrees. You would really have to be a believer to put up a stand for every wind. In my younger years, I solved that problem by carrying a plywood crotch stand on my back, shinnying up the tree, and tying it off, but no more. It is too dangerous! Besides you have to be half squirrel! At first, I expected my two sons to do it, but they struggled. But when the grandchildren came, well, in came the tree stands. And who uses them? Yes, and I don't feel guilty at all!

I believe I have tried most every way there is to hunt whitetails with a bow. For me there is no way so dependable or predictable as bed hunting even with its shortcomings. Is it a guarantee to success? No, but it does guarantee many more lessons learned and many more hours of watching deer up close. Here I was having killed two nice bucks in two years. Was it luck, persistence, or were the beds the way to go? Well, the next year I found there were still more important lessons to be learned as you will see in the next story.

Hunting the peak of the rut for a beekeeper can be a battle of priorities. The hives need to be weighed, fed, and insulated for winter. In 1983, the third year of learning beds, I was not able to put all of my energy to bow hunting until Thanksgiving week. On Tuesday morning, I was about to learn a couple more lessons.

Even though all of my bee work was not done, I was sitting in a good bed. By 9 o'clock the responsibility of my bee work got the best of me and I slid down out of my tree. Half way down the hill, I crossed a well-used path with a big track in it. I'd missed it on the way up in the dark. Thinking this might make a good evening stand using downhill thermals, I spotted a half blown down oak on the downwind side. Deciding to check it out, I climbed up, pulling my bow up as an afterthought.

Fifteen minutes of sitting made me feel confident in the spot. Just as I was about to lower my bow, a doe went streaking by with a one-year-old buck hot on her trail. He was met by a three-year-old that took up the chase running her to the bed I'd just left! No sooner was he out of sight when a 160 class nine point came from the direction the doe had come from. He stopped six yards out on the other side of a cedar tree. He wanted to know why the year-old buck was getting nervous from my wind. I spotted a small opening in the branches behind the shoulder and drew back while he watched the little buck. When I fired, he just walked away. He didn't even flinch! After two more arrows clattered through the prickly ash, I sat back totally demoralized. How could I have missed a shot that close? Staring at the space between the branches, I spotted a straight stick out of place on the ground. It was red. My arrows were green! Tying the tether string to the bow was difficult with a pair of shaking hands. The blood trail was easy to follow, but when I jumped him 200 yards out, I figured it to be a liver shot. Resisting the temptation to follow, I went home and tried to relax for three hours before enlisting Kathy's help. He ended up going another 250 yards. It was the biggest deer I'd ever shot.

Some of you by now have guessed at least one of the lessons of that morning. The first is about that 9 o'clock hour. In the years to come I became convinced that during the rut, rush hour in the woods comes roughly between 9:00 and 10:00. Not that I would want to miss the half hour on either side of sun up, but I really don't want to miss rush hour! The other lesson is, depending on several factors, Thanksgiving week can be a wild time in the woods.

Staying with the rush hour idea, I would like to fast forward a few years. I don't remember the exact year but I knew we were approaching the peak of the rut at or near November 10. I also knew that coaching high school wrestling was cutting into my bee work not to mention my bow hunting. At 8:15 in the morning I'm in my bee house loading my truck for winterizing my bees. The phone rings and it's the athletic director from the high school. "Bob, why are you not in your tree?" "Because I've been spending too much time in the wrestling room and I'm buried", I answered. "Then unbury yourself and get out in the woods. The deer are going nuts!" She was in her tractor hauling corn for her husband.

Though my neighbors might disagree, I do try to be responsible when it comes to my bees. Being so far behind with bee work I had decided to wait for Thanksgiving week, and then get really serious. But she sounded so emphatic that I had to believe something special was going on. I thanked her and told her I would try. Wow! I had never tried anything like this before. I ran to the house and jumped in the shower. Out in the barrel shed (the place where we store our honey), I put on my outer clothes and boots, fired one practice shot and tried not to run to the woods. Figuring the rut must be peaked, I decided to forego the classic bed stand and headed for a place I call the court yard where I had seen several does get bred. It was low, had flowing water, plenty of cover but not too much, and today the wind was just right.

I had settled into the stand less than 15 minutes; it was 9:15. All at once from the ridge top near a bed I heard, not the classic grunt, but a loud beller, almost like a cow! Suddenly, down the hill came a doe followed by a beautiful eleven point. Behind them were three small bucks. She took him right past me at 15 yards. He looked right up at me but was so preoccupied with the other bucks that he just kept coming. It was easy! It was the second biggest buck I'd ever shot. So, does that mean you don't have to get up in the dark and be at your stand by first light? I wouldn't push my luck. In this case, there was a whole lot of just that, LUCK!!

It was in these early years that one of my most important lessons was taught to me by a doe with a fawn. I had been scouting a patch of large cedar trees and could see that the deer were spending a lot of time in them. Deer love cedars for several reasons. When the snow gets too deep to dig for food, that's where they will be. And though they love the cedars for beds, it is not the easiest set up for getting a clear shot. You plan to take them on the very downwind edge. That is how it was this day, and I found the perfect tree for a north wind with the grove slopping to the south. Checking the tree out, I noticed a pesky limb hanging over a good path heading into the bed. As I left the stand, I went over to the smaller tree with the troublesome limb, shinnied up the tree, pulled the folding saw out of my boot, and lopped it off. Then I slid back down. That next day the wind was wrong for that bed and I went somewhere else. Two days later, the wind came almost back to the north, so I decided to sit at my cedar bed. I was in the tree at first light and it wasn't long when a doe and a fawn came right up the path. She missed my wind, but when she got near the small tree I had climbed 2 days earlier to cut off the limb, she went nuts! Putting her nose on the tree she stretched her neck up as far as she could. Then she proceeded to stomp and let everyone know that the bougie man had come to her bed! She finally left and I decided to set it out. Not surprising, nothing came. This kind of experience can let the air out of your tires, but it goes to show how scent can linger and how careful you must be! More on this later.

First buck taken in a bed

Rush hour buck

Chapter 2: Recognizing the Bed

"Walk through life as if you have something to learn, and you will"

Vernon Howard

To be clear, when we talk about bed hunting, we are talking about the doe beds. The idea of trying to take a mature buck in his own bed is just short of impossible. Except during the peak of the rut, he will almost always be bedded before first light. His home bed will be in the thickest cover he can find. If he doesn't hear you, he will smell you. Well, you might say, just go after him in a high wind and stay on the downwind side.   The fact is that in high winds your scent will swirl. With high winds, they are constantly alert. I believe it is draining on them. Besides, a couple of times of that and you may push him out of your territory.

Thankfully, the does prefer a more open cover for bedding. This is not to say that when being pursued by a buck before she is "ready", she may crawl into a place that a rabbit might struggle with. I once saw a doe jump into a wood pile to get away from a pursuing buck only to have the buck jump on top of the pile to flush her out! It didn't work. She wouldn't move. The poor guy ran off to find someone more accommodating.

I have a doe bed with a big patch of multiflora rose on the far side. The does don't spend a lot of time in the multiflora, but often the bucks will come by following the does. When the does bed down, the bucks wander over and lie down in it and seem right at home in the multiflora. This past season, I shot a coyote there and made a good hit. It jumped into the multiflora leaving a good blood trail. Try as I might, I could not follow him. The thorny branches were too much. There is an old church song with a verse that goes "Through thorny ways leads to a joyful end". Whoever wrote that must not have experienced multiflora rose!

Once when I was looking for new beds, I climbed a long hill and as it happened, the wind was just right. As I reached the crest I found some extra heavy cover. Saying to myself,

"Wow! If I were a buck, I would be right…" My eyes met his and a three-year-old buck jumped up and away. Where was the wind? It was coming from behind him over the ridge and straight at me. He saw me, that was part of his safety plan!

In Northeast Iowa during the month of November, the predominant winds are West and Northwest followed by Southwest. East winds are harder to come by. Stand for stand, there is more action with an East wind, probably because it means that a storm is coming and the barometer is dropping. But more time is spent in Westerly wind beds simply because there are just more west winds. In the old days, I would run to the top of the hill near our house to feel the wind direction, then go back in the house and write my wife a note to tell her where I was going. Now I still write a note but I can usually get the direction off of the computer, and also where and when the wind is going to switch. One thing about computer forecasts, they have improved tremendously, but they don't seem to be able to pick up winds less than three mph. A bed hunter may throw up his hands when he sees "calm winds". This is usually not how it is. A wind of one or two mph is still a wind and the deer depend on it. However, you may not be able to sense the direction unless you find yourself an unobstructed location, preferably high and walk a few steps in each direction. Leaving your hood loose helps scoop the air and give you a better idea of where it is coming from. A one or two mph wind may mean the wind is getting ready to switch. Looking ahead on the forecast may tell you that. Checking the maps of high and low pressures can also help, given clockwise winds on the highs and counterclockwise winds on the lows. This will give you an idea of a coming barometric change. The deer won't be sitting quite so still on low pressures. All this keeps us tuned into the natural world and what Mother Nature is up to.

Though I don't usually count individual beds within a bedding area, it might not be a bad idea as a confidence booster. A fresh snow can be a big help as long as you keep in mind the wind direction right after the snow. Another thing to keep in mind while bed hunting is that just after the gun season what you see might not be the usual routine in the deer world. Their world has been turned upside down and may not go back to normal for some time. Also, the weather is often deteriorating and their natural inclination to yard up is occurring. It is at these times that I tend to back off on the pressure I put on them as it seems they may be under enough stress as it is. I guess I have memories of what happened to herd numbers after some really bad winters. But I'm saving that for another chapter.

As hinted at in the previous chapter, doe beds are usually just downwind of the crest of the ridge with the wind perpendicular to the ridgeline. It needs good cover but not as heavy as a mature buck. The higher the wind the farther down the slope they will bed, up to about 10 mph. When the wind velocity exceeds that, depending on how much windbreak is upwind of the bed, they may not want that bed at all.

Geography and topography play an important part in bed location. There are two situations that would be good to pay particular attention to. It took me quite a few years to realize just how important they are. One situation could be called the point bedding area. The other could be called the round top. The point bed will usually have a ravine on each side of the point and can be used for winds from nearly 180 degrees of the compass. The round top is a raised area sloping on all sides for 360-degree wind direction. The deer will only pick one spot per wind direction to bed in that bedding area, but they seem to be more comfortable and frequent these places more. Be careful not to overuse places like these! Stand placement can get tricky in these locations.

I have helped other bow hunters find bedding areas and usually end up feeling envious. Many bow hunters will hunt for years without realizing that they are very close to some of the finest bedding areas I have ever seen! Once, after several successful seasons, a good friend and traditional bow hunter with far more experience than I, asked if he could see one of my set ups. Choosing my most favorite and most inaccessible spots, we climbed the long steep slope to the bed. As he stood in the middle of it, he turned and said to me, "Bob, this place does nothing for me!" I realized then that bed hunting was something new.

At this point it would be well to talk about overhunting your beds. Early in the season you can get by with more mistakes in the form of residual scent, poor stand placement, or an intruding approach to the stand. If I were to rank any of these chapters needed for success, number one would be without a doubt "Our World of Smells", followed by "The Ghost in the Wilderness". Don't let them know you've been there!

All day buck

Chapter 3: Our World of Smells

"Let us permit nature to have her way. She understands her business better than we do." Michael de Montaigne

Veteran hunters have told me that the coyote surpasses the whitetail in smell ability. I'm not so sure. Actually, we shouldn't get careless with either one. In their own way, and the raccoon as well, these animals will tell you when you need to improve your hygiene. We leave our scent in the woods in several ways. Obviously, the track of our boots can give us away. But our bibs, coat, hat, gloves, and of course our skin can all pollute our hunting area. I've tried coveralls that hold in the scent, and they are an improvement. But going out twice a day for days on end puts a scent load of any clothing simply because we are not going to wash them every time we go out. I'm always amazed at the way my Labrador greets me when I've been to another person's house or around another dog. Though we cannot smell those odors, they are very real and can be very persistent. There is nothing more disturbing than to think you've got everything right, just to have a doe with her fawn come in and tell everyone around that "someone has been sleeping in my bed".

One of the most polluting sources we have is our very own breath, and most hunters don't talk about it or deal with it. I first started realizing this when watching deer cross my path. Even though all my clothes had been freshly washed in earth soap and the outer layers stored in a building totally inert of any human scent, the deer would stop and smell the leaves and the bark of the trees several feet from my path. In my early years, that was all they needed to turn and walk away. Now, for the most part, they usually take notice but keep on coming.

But when I heard that Native Americans would refrain from eating meat before hunting deer, I had to give it a try. I told an old game warden friend of mine about my plan. He said that by the end of the season, I wouldn't be able to climb my tree. Turned out he was right! So now I just cut back on the meat and I believe it helps.

And now once again you are thinking that this guy is on the fringes. All I can tell you is that something is working! For the morning hunt I eat no breakfast but carb load the night before. I have to have something in my pocket to get through rush hour. That used to be a peanut butter sandwich, but after many bad experiences trying to eat something that heavy on stand with bedded deer ten to fifteen yards out, I went to dried apples. When deer bed in front of you, they plan to be there for the day. Old does will stand for fifteen to twenty minutes in the middle of the bed gathering all the smells that the wind will provide before she lays down. If you've placed your stand properly, she will be upwind. Good luck with the discipline it takes to stay still. You may find yourself wishing for a buck or a coyote to come along to push her out. But to expect the wind to stay steady for seven to eight hours is asking too much. Even during a two hour watch she will get a wisp of wind from your direction and you don't want it carrying something strong enough to set her off. Keep in mind that the slope behind you will have thermals coming up and at her, competing with the prevailing wind of the day. Your hope is that those thermals will be pushed up and away by the prevailing wind before they get to your bedded deer.

At the end of the last chapter is a classic picture of a three-year-old buck bedded ten yards behind me, downwind of my stand in heavy cover, watching the deep valley below. It was the Tuesday before Thanksgiving. He had been watching a group of nine does and fawns with a bigger ten point by his side. I was so busy photographing the does that I did not see the two bucks underneath me. A moment after realizing they were there, I stood with the bow in one hand and the camera in the other, trying to decide if the ten was big enough. By the time I got it sorted out in my head, I was left with one overexposed shot of the ten-point, as he melted into the herd, and they did not appreciate his company. The eight point then bedded down behind me at eight-thirty. I had not intended to stay all day and did not bring anything to eat or drink. But all this activity was too much to turn my back on. The buck stayed all day until 3:30, getting up twice to check out incoming does and then went right back to the same spot to bed. The picture tells a lot. He is lying in a spot at the farthest downwind part of the bed on the edge of a ridge that is exactly perpendicular to the wind of that day. This is not just coincidence. He is also in the heaviest cover that the immediate area provides, but is still able to view the huge valley below. He would be able to see me getting into an evening stand 200 yards below that is nestled in a grove of red oaks that I use when the acorns are falling. But rest assured that I would not be using that stand when the wind is out of the Southwest as it was this day. The fact that he or the rest of the herd did not smell me could be reassuring, but one must never let down your guard. Experiences like this make the constant vigilance of scent control worth it.   There was a ship in the squadron I served in whose motto was on a patch worn on the jackets of the sailors that went, "Semper Vigilantes", i.e. "Always Vigilant"! That needs to be us.

Growing up on a farm, my job after school in winter was to feed the cows while my dad milked. There were two rows of eleven cows with their heads facing each other with a feeding alley in the middle. First, they all got a big scoop of corn silage, then a pail of ground corn topped off with a small pail of malted barley. My father was a nutrition fanatic. By the time I threw down the alfalfa hay from the mow above, the cows had most of the feed already in their stomachs. I would spread the hay out and they would grab the slices and shake them apart, belching as they went, obviously in cow heaven. The smell was intoxicating!

Though we are not ruminants, I don't believe breakfast or a peanut butter sandwich will go unnoticed. There are times when you can definitely get by without going to extremes with scent control. Early season will be less of a problem, but in these days with ever increasing hunting pressure, it doesn't take long. At the peak of the rut, they obviously have other things on their minds, but I've seen does in heat that seem to have their noses supercharged. Later in the season you will need all of your ducks in a row. Very dry or extreme cold will help us some. Warm damp weather in the later season will really test you. It would seem prudent then to just start the season right out with the best scent control routine that works for you.

There is no greater test of a father's patience than trying to get your young hunter into the woods by first light when so many of their priorities seem to come before getting ready to go to the woods clean and scent free. But then nothing is more gratifying than to see tradition being handed down as you help them drag out their first buck!

There are so many details when it comes to mitigating odor. In setting up a stand we need to realize that we will smell to some extent and therefore must do the best we can with stand location. We can't always have a cliff on the downwind side. We also have to get close enough to where the deer will be. Wind currents are a science. Some setups are pretty reliable because of the surrounding terrain. Others will fishtail the winds constantly. Winds above ten mph are never dependable. Try as you might, you will never know for sure until you set the stand. Your teachers will let you know how well the stand is placed.

One particular stand that baffles me is one of my courting yards, as I like to call them, where I've seen multiple does come to get bred. It is at the junction of two ravines with springs flowing in each one. It is about eighty yards in from the edge of the woods where the springs flow into an open grassy valley. This kind of setup would usually have the wind pushing and pulling back and forth constantly. For whatever reason, the deer almost never smell me in that stand. This is not a classic bed location but works well with higher winds morning or evening, and especially at the peak of the rut. On one occasion in the nineties near the end of the season, fourteen does and fawns moved in on me completely surrounding this stand and none of them seemed to know I was there!

The classic bed, as I have described, makes the wind problem much easier to resolve. If the wind is less than ten mph and steady, the only real problems are your approach, and if the area downwind of the stand is such that the deer want to check it out before they bed. If your downwind side is steep, there is less tendency for them to be there unless their food source is in that direction. Does usually come into the beds WITH the wind. They want to know what is behind them. Bucks will usually come in CROSSWIND unless following the does. But if your downwind side is not steep, he can very often come straight at you into YOUR wind. This is when you hope the sun is up creating a strong thermal lifting your scent over him. As you can see or already know, there are a lot of factors and many are variable. Keeping our scent below their alarm threshold will MAKE IT EASY!

By now you are no doubt wondering if all this planning is worth it. Some may even be a bit overwhelmed. But I would just like everyone to know that this style of bow hunting has worked very well for me and the few hunters I know who have tried it. Some might say that you don't want to put up a stand for every wind direction. I can understand that. But next time you want to move a stand that hasn't produced, put it on a bed – with someone to help you, and wait for the wind to come around.

I would like to tell a story of what happened when everything was just right. I use the word WAS because I don't think it will happen again given the herd dynamics that have come about after the nineties. It is a story about a bed hunt about 1992 that took place near the end of the season. Remembering the bed, I can tell you that it was a Southwest wind that day. I had only a few days left in the November season but the way things were going I was in no hurry to fill my tag with a small deer. Snow was on the ground but not deep. Just after first light, the deer started moving in, a doe and fawn first followed by young bucks that just kept coming and coming. The doe and fawn did not stay with all that company. The bucks started bedding down one by one. Before 9:00 I had eight bucks scattered throughout the bed with more coming in. Some got up and wandered around. There was a steep hill behind me so nobody got downwind. I could not tell if the ones that wandered away had come back, but I guessed there were twelve all together and not a three-year-old buck in the bunch. It was mind boggling! No surprise that no more does came in. But that was the nineties. Now I get almost as many zeroes as multiple deer in the beds. I'm sure it is better this way, less disease and depredation. I had not gotten into carrying a camera then as I do now. That would have been a classic.

Who's there?

Chapter 4: The Ghost in the Wilderness

"If you truly love nature, you will find beauty everywhere" Laura Ingalls Wilder

I was about 6 years old when my father first took me squirrel hunting. His first words whispered as we entered the woods were "Try to be quiet and still. There are probably six pairs of eyes watching us!" That must have been a teachable moment and I never forgot it.   Yet I've violated that rule so many times and watched as the white flags bound away. The morning hunt however, puts timing on our side. If we enter the woods at just the point where you can see branches three feet ahead, there will be less stumbling and crashing. The deer will mostly be still feeding. I carry a small light for safety thinking the deer should not be there anyway. If your set up is good on the bed, they should not smell you. Your trip home should stay away from other beds for that wind. So theoretically, you could come and go without the deer knowing you were there except for the lingering scent which by evening (if you've worked on the scent problem) will have mostly dissipated.

However, there is one problem I've faced multiple times and usually it makes me smile. Suppose one or multiple deer have decided that the bed you have chosen is where they want to spend the day! If you simply climb down after the morning rush hour, there will be a major exit and it won't be pretty. In this situation I have tried about everything. Depending on how determined they are to stay, it can get really interesting. A practice arrow in front of their nose works sometimes. Throwing your folding saw or apple does not work well. Letting your bow down and swinging it from side to side gets some interesting reactions. A grunt call or a rattle risks them looking up at you. If you truly want to slip away unnoticed it can be a real problem. Whatever you do, less is better. You want them to come back again. In the old days I would slip around the back of the tree and slide carefully to the ground. They usually would leave but not with much fanfare. With tree stands there is only one way out safely!

Mostly because of the cold, I don't do well sitting completely motionless. I try to blend in well with my tree and take note of the background. Hanging cedar branches around me helps. A face mask, gillie hat, well blending camo all help. The woods creatures will let you know how you are doing. Your tree should not sit by itself if possible unless it is a monster bur oak with multiple limbs. Background is key.

Many squirrels have sniffed my boots. One climbed the trunk behind me and then jumped on my gillie hat and started digging for a nut! He gave up before he knew what he had! Once as I held the bow waiting for an approaching buck, a small flock of chickadees flew around me with one landing on my arrow. It spotted the colored pins on my sight and had to hop along the arrow to check them out. The scariest experience of all was one morning when I had gotten to my stand early and was congratulating myself on my timing when a very large barred owl flew into the tree next to me. He immediately starred straight at me. I turned my head away to look up the valley from where he had come. I turned back just in time to see cupped wings and outstretched talons six feet away! I ducked as he sailed passed! These are stories I use in hunter safety classes when the kids get bored. It works well when you dress for the occasion.

Turkeys are about the greatest challenge for remaining unseen. I find the best way for a fresh Thanksgiving bird is to let the whole flock of pullets go by and then take the last one. Toms will really test you. I tend to use darker colored arrows just because of them, but that makes seeing where you hit a deer more difficult. Several times I've crawled into my stand at first light and hear putting in the same tree over my head. Only once did I have one fly down close enough to zap. That was a successful hunt!

Many hunters will say that the woodlot whitetail adjusts to being disturbed by human pressure and may just be more wary when he comes back again. To that I would say yes, but a four-year-old or older buck will adjust by coming back when you are not there – in the middle of the night, if he comes back at all. Minimizing your disturbance is all important if you want a chance at mature bucks. It is better if they don't know about the ghost in the wilderness.

Many of my bow hunting friends and I have come to the conclusion that the four-year-old buck becomes a different animal when he survives his 3rd season with antlers. Not to take anything away from the younger buck's ability to sense danger, but the older deer seem to know how to stay out of trouble. He takes wariness to a whole new level. We will cover more on that later.

I think I saw a ghost!

Is someone watching us?

Chapter 5: Calculating the Rut

"If one way be better than another, that you may be sure is nature's way"
Aristotle

The whitetail rut has been the subject of many wildlife studies and experiments. Many of these have much data upon which to draw their conclusions. When you look at the big picture, it would appear that how a rut plays out is definitely not just what happens in the months of October, November, or December. A given rut starts to be set up at least a full year before. If you live in northern states, winters can be formidable. Later in this book are some stories of winters of my youth that are in the history books. They happened at a time when food plots and deer management practices were much different. But even today they can leave their mark on the deer herd.

In spring, predators can have a serious impact on fawn survival. We live in coyote country, and though I love to hear them howl, I never pass up a chance to zap one. They are really hard on fawns.

Drought can increase the incidence of blue tongue and EHD, spread by midges and is fatal soon after symptoms occur. Deer will congregate at water sources to relieve the thirst which comes with the disease.

A full moon in the middle of October with clear skies, low winds, and low temperatures can accelerate the rut. Although most of the activity will be at night, sunrise and sunset will get more exciting. Midday activity might not seem to change much but keep in mind the amount of cover in the form of standing corn and tall native grasses of the CRP (Conservation Reserve Program) fields may hide what is really going on.

A full moon around October 22nd gets the rut moving and puts the dark of the moon just before the peak of the November rut around the 11th. I am a Navy veteran, so around Veteran's Day whenever someone is kind enough to thank me for my service, I just say thank you, and if it is okay, I'm going to spend the whole day in the woods. During the November peak, lots of quiet cloudy days with a falling barometer make the rut really go. Winds should be less than 10 mph. An early corn harvest puts more deer in the woods and a good buck to doe ratio makes the big guys search a little harder. All this being said, the truth is you never know for sure! Try not to let all you read or hear lead you down that primrose path to disappointment.

Sorting all of these factors out is pretty difficult, but the result comes down to just one thing – SIGN! My favorites are big tracks with dew claws and shredded trees. The best time to be checking is October, keeping in mind that the sign will become exponential as the weeks go by. Once October comes to an end, I do not think it is a good idea to continue tromping through the woods looking for all of the sign you can discover. Just going to and from your favorite set ups with your eyes wide open should give you an idea of what is happening. You can drive the big guys right out of your woods – at least in the daylight, with too much of your presence.

When talking about the rutting activity, we can only talk in generalities realizing that so many factors are involved. Mother Nature has her own schedule and it can be quite different than what we think it should be.

One year at or about November 10th the wind was blowing at 15-20 mph. In the middle of the day, I asked my thirteen-year-old son, Mat, if he would help me move some stands to more strategic places. I told him there would be no need to take our bows as the deer would be laying low with the strong wind. As you might guess, they were chasing all over the place seemingly oblivious of our presence.

Then there was another year when I was sitting over one of my favorite beds feeling guiltier by the minute that I had not a single bee hive ready for winter. There had been very little activity for days from what I figured was the full moon. At 9:00 AM, the beginning of rush hour, my guilt overcame me and I slid down my tree and headed home. Reaching the edge of the woods, I heard a doe charging behind me and almost ran me over! Knowing something would be coming, I knocked an arrow just as a nice three-year-old buck went flying by and jumped the fence into a picked corn field. A loud "meahh" made him stop and look back. A heart shot put him down with a somersault in less than 50 yards.

One month ago, we were finishing up the Thanksgiving peak of the rut which at one time I thought I had all figured out. However, in the last years, that has changed for a variety of reasons, probably first on the list being hunting pressure. Moon phase cannot be the problem multiple years in a row. But it is hard to give up on that part of the rut that has provided me with so many opportunities at big bucks.

Maybe one more reality story is in order. On the Friday after Thanksgiving, my 30- year-old son, Mat, who gave up teaching and coaching in Southern Iowa to come home and become a beekeeper, asked me which one of our stands would be best for a Southwest wind. This was November 27th, two days ahead of a full moon. I told him to try the place we called the delta peak where two deep valleys straddle a high ridge. I reminded him about the moon and that there had been very little activity for a week. At 7:15 AM, a 7 ½ year old came marching up the steep hill into the bed right under Mat. A double lung shot put him down in 40 yards but he got up and went another 80 yards to the neighbor's fence. Not wanting to disturb my hunt he dragged that deer one third of a mile (by GPS) back to the truck and loaded it himself! That deer had one of the largest bodies I have ever seen! I'm sure adrenaline was a factor and the long downhill direction towards the truck from the bed probably helped, but even in my finest day, I could not have done that. The deer had a 21" spread, 29" neck measured on the outside, two broken tines, and essentially no teeth! The old boy was probably visiting my neighbor's cash of does that hung close to his food plot. He was probably heading to his own bed by way of one more doe bed, just a little too late!

It is human nature to want to have it all figured out. Truth is we will spend a lot of time trying. This year marks my 50th year of bow hunting and I feel there is much more to learn, partially because so many things keep changing. A good friend of mine, a traditional bow hunter and gifted taxidermist, keeps telling me after every little secret we learn that," Now it will be easy!" We both laugh every time we say it. The fact of the matter is you still have to get out of bed in the dark and be settled in by first light, then be able to sit for 3 ½ to 4 hours. If your only motivation is to kill a big buck, then you could be setting yourself up for disappointment. Bow hunting is tough, but I consider it therapeutic.

The Rut is on!

Chapter 6: The Extra Mile

"Heaven is under our feet as well as over our heads." Henry David Thoreau

This chapter's title sheds light in at least three different ways that one's confidence and immersing oneself into the many aspects of hunting whitetails with a bow can draw you in despite hardship.

The first story goes way back to around 1987 when bow hunting was much different for many reasons. It is a story from the past when attitudes and perspectives about hunting were not as they are today. I feel blessed to have lived through those times. Never wanting to disturb the woods any more than necessary for myself or anyone else, I always left the freezer deer for the last week of the season. Often this plan would put the pressure on as the proverbial clock ticked down. In a previous chapter, I wrote about backtracking a nice buck only to have another buck come into a doe bed that I was checking out. Snow at the end of November doesn't always happen, but when it does, it is a gift to bow hunters that is seldom made use of. This story brings a lot of elements together and just retelling it evokes a powerful feeling of nostalgia that makes me thankful I became a bow hunter.

I was by a bed on a ridge overlooking the river with the snow coming down. It was 10 o'clock and at the end of that watch, and only two days left in the November season. It had been an exciting season but I had still not connected. As I watched the snow pile up, I thought about that first time that I backtracked a buck and how I found multiple beds in the process. So down the tree I slid and started looking for a big track. It didn't take long. Hoping my wife wouldn't worry I headed out through the hills like Jeremiah Johnson with a bow. I reasoned that the track must be fresh and the big boy had not spent much time in any one place or the track would be covered up. Thankfully, the snow started letting up or I'd have lost it. The backtracking took me through a couple of beds but they didn't afford me that perfect tree. At a fence line I stopped to think it over. I had no idea whose land was on the other side. I did not want to become known as a trespasser. Yet, there was something to be learned here. There were no cell phones those days and, given the prevailing attitude about bow hunting, I did not think I would be bothering anybody. I proceeded figuring I'd check out the plat book that night and call around to determine the landowner. As it was by that afternoon I had gone through several farms before I found the perfect set up. It was a bed for a Northeast wind that was blowing softly now. A doe and fawn jumped out, and there was the perfect tree. Trying to keep track of where I had been and where I was, I had made nearly a full circle not far from the road where the truck was parked. As soon as I got home, I pulled out the plat book to see where my exploring had taken me and who the landowner was. Recognizing one of the names as a family whose land I had beehives on, I called them to ask who owned the land where my set up was. "Don't worry," he said. "The guy doesn't live around here and he doesn't hunt." I told him I'd get the guy some honey.

The next morning the wind was still out of the Northeast. I started the climb to the ridgetop with my plywood stand on my back wishing I had put the stand in when I was at the tree the day before. But not knowing whose land I was on or if the wind would hold, I opted not to. Shinnying up, I jammed the crotch stand in and was starting to tie it off when in the early light, I spotted a doe with her fawn coming through the snow on my trail. Mama was obviously not happy, sticking her nose in my footsteps, and peering around nervously. Every time she would look away, I would pull my bow up slowly. Everything was secure, but she was getting pretty worked up. I was praying for a distraction that soon came in the form of a year-old buck who was taking an interest in her fawn who had wandered out crosswind about 20 yards. Knowing that the track that took me to this place was from a big deer, but also knowing that there was no meat in the freezer, I decided that this buck was a bird in hand and surely was worth more than a bigger one in the bush. Having the bow at full anchor, I spotted a movement behind the young buck. It was a nicer two-year-old, so I eased up and watched him move in. Before I could get drawn back on him, Mr. Big showed up and my heart maxed out! He headed right for the fawn who didn't know what to do with all of the attention but stood her ground. As I was about to draw, the old buck snapped his head up, obviously smelling something. Instead of leaving he came straight for my tree and put his nose to the bark. I remember the difficulty of making a vertical shot especially with mama behind me. When I released, he jumped and then walked slowly around my tree. As I frantically got another arrow knocked, he coughed and I relaxed. He walked ten yards out, laid down, stretched out his head and it was over. He was a beautiful 15 point non-typical. I remembered him from a previous year in a different bed. He had walked right under me, but I clinked the bow taking it off the hanger.

Leaning back against the tree, I had to just take it all in for a while as I viewed the beautiful river bottom below. An overwhelming feeling of gratitude came over me as I thought about all the things that, in one way or another, had led me to this point in my life. My parents and the small farm life, my wife who puts up with all of my crazy dreams, and on and on. These are the things that shape our values and inspire us to put in the extra effort that makes life worth living.

I never went back to that place. The next year, the land was sold and the new owners became part of the new wave of deer hunting. But I was so blessed to have hunted at a time when life seemed so much freer.

Staying with the theme of limits, I have a couple of tales that should remind us of how important it is to listen to our bodies, and stay in the best shape we can. In that regard, there should be no argument that we can all do better. This probably sounds like a speech from a coach standing on the wrestling mat watching the tongues hang out of all of his wrestlers. And that is where I was for 28 years. I liked to think it helped me in the woods, which it did but not in every way. I also like to think that I might have kept a few of them out of prison, but I'll never know. The time involved was a struggle and, just as serious, the smell of the wrestling room could not be covered up or scrubbed off! But I would not have traded the experiences for anything.

In the fall of 1985, there were two nice bucks roaming my neighbor's woods that local bow hunters were quite excited about. They called one Tall Rack and the other Wide Rack. One day in mid-October, my dad called and asked if we could do a float trip down the river for some Canadas. As an old Navy pilot, though he loved the woods, wing shooting was in his soul. We headed out with our canoe made into a floating blind. He was in the bow with his Browning 12 Gauge automatic and I was in the stern. I pushed hard because I wanted to do an evening stand. The geese weren't down yet, but it was a nice float.

The place I had in mind for my evening stand was at the bottom of a wooded hill with a bed on top and at the opposite end of the territory that other hunters were in. At the base of the hill was a wooded ravine that was starting to get torn up. The approach was a rolling pasture with grass one inch tall from the effects of a dry fall. I was late and hurrying across the field when, just before topping the last hill in the pasture, I spotted a deer at the base of the woods leading up to the bed. Putting my spotting scope on it, I thought to myself, "That looks like a buck but he must have his head down between two bull thistles." Then he raised his head and I saw that the "thistles" were attached to his head! It was freakish! The main beams went straight up with points in all directions. Immediately I knelt down which put him out of sight. There was nothing I could do except get ready. When I saw the antlers coming over the hill I drew back. By the time he got within 30 yards, he knew something was wrong. He looked straight at me but all I had was the front of his chest. No way could I try that. He took a giant leap and stopped 40 yards out broadside. I had never shot a deer at that distance. At the time I was shooting a 70# Jennings T-Star that shot 180 ft/second which is quite different than the 320 ft/second bow that I shoot now.

I had been practicing a lot, so in a weak moment I decided to try it. In my memory, I watched the arrow as if it was in slow motion head right where I was aiming but by the time it got there, Tall Rack had made two jumps and was nowhere near the arrow. I was actually relieved that it was a clean miss. I never saw him the rest of the season nor the next. But the following year I was scouting a woods three miles from that spot and there he was standing at the downwind edge of a woods in a clearing. Looking through my spotting scope I had to say out loud, "So this is where you have been hiding." He was even more magnificent than my first encounter. I never heard of someone getting him. Most of the local deer hunters at the time would call me up for a measuring score if they had anything unusual. My hope was that he lived out his life in obscurity passing along his unusual genetics, although I never did see anything quite like him again.

That year we had expanded our bee business and the extra work competed with my woods time. By Thanksgiving I was back in the woods again most every day, but winter was moving in. The Sunday after Thanksgiving I woke up to 6 degrees and a stiff Northwest wind. For some reason I was needed at church that morning, but not until 10 o'clock. I headed out to a bed in the woods, that 20 years later we would own. As I crawled into my stand overlooking the open valley of tall big bluestem, I saw a deer in a picked corn field at the timber's edge and next to a creek that flowed through the valley. With my spotting scope, I saw his head muzzling through the snowy cornstalks. I remember wondering if those were stalks or antlers by his head. Then he raised his head and my heart went into overdrive. It was Wide Rack! He fed for what seemed like forever. I kept my finger tab hand in my pocket, but my bow hand was already frozen. Finally, his head came up and he hurried straight into the wind towards the bed. As he marched slowly through the woods, I thought about an old trapper who always counted on extreme cold to hide his scent, but I wasn't too sure about that. He came almost to the bed and then turned so as to skirt it downwind. He was now in my wind at 20 yards moving to my right. I drew back, forgetting that the extra layers of clothes always made me shoot left. The arrow hit 4 inches back from where I wanted. He bailed out, down through the trees and out into the open valley. Two hundred yards out the he laid down, then got up and laid down again. I watched for another 15 minutes trying to thaw out the frost bit fingers on both hands. His head stayed up, so I decided to leave him until after church. The way home was painful, but I knew I had to keep moving my hands.

What the sermon was about I had no clue, and we did not stop at the grocery store on the way home! Kathy came with me to the woods and at the bed, I crawled back up the tree for a look. His head was down; he was dead. It had been a lung shot, but pretty far back. The valley that he crossed was planted to walnuts that next spring with the help of the Forestry Service. Now that valley is solid trees over 30 feet tall. The bed above them that I hunted that morning has been one of my all-time favorites. Every time I sit it and look at the valley below, I marvel at what can be done for habitat with a little planning and care.

Staying with the extra effort theme, I have one more saga to tell that you may not believe and I can't blame you if you don't. You just have to keep in mind that it took place in the nineties when the deer herd was exploding, and I was probably in the best physical shape of my life. It was January 10th, the last day of the last season and there was no venison in our freezer. It was 10 degrees with a brutal Northwest wind and we had just had an ice storm on top of 10 inches of snow. Heading to the stand, breaking through the ice with each step, I was sure that no deer would come with all that noise. Apparently, the deer were feeding far enough away and didn't hear my

crunching. I found my tree in the dark.
Thankfully the ice only covered one side of the tree's trunk and I was able dig into the bark of the old Ash tree with my fingers, knees, and insteps of my boots. It took what I thought was all I had to make it to the crotch 20 feet up. I jammed the plywood stand into the crotch and tied it off. As I started to pull the bow up, I realized that my line was tangled in some vines. Short of damaging the bow, I could not pull it up! So, yes, I slid back down the tree, untangled the bow, and climbed back up! That DID take everything I had. No sooner had I caught my breath when I heard the sound of approaching deer. It was unnerving as each hoof broke through the ice. Fourteen deer came in and bedded down in front of me, but not one antler in the bunch. All were bedding upwind with the closest about 8 yards out. I decided to wait it out. At that time, and still today I find it difficult to shoot a doe even though in those days it would have been the wisest thing to do given the exploding numbers. It was probably why I was in that situation as the buck/doe ratio was totally askew.

Anyway, for the next three hours I watched the deer react to all of the sounds in the woods with the ice cracking and creaking. The sun peaked out and I maneuvered my boots into its warmth to thaw my frozen feet. Finally, at 10 o'clock, from across the ravine came the unmistakable sound of an approaching deer. It was a three-year-old 4x4. He cross-winded into the bed, walked to the upper end, and disappeared. Did he bed? I could not tell. All eyes had been on him but nobody got up. I decided to wait. At noon the town whistle blew and he stood up, then laid right back down. Ok, I'll wait until 2 o'clock but then I'd have to head home to thaw out before wrestling practice. Sometime around 1:30 my head started spinning. My carb loading from the night before was gone, so I slowly pulled out my sandwich and began to chew. Suddenly, as had happened so many times before when eating on stand with bedded deer and gusty winds, the oldest doe jumped to her feet obviously alarmed. Everyone else just looked at her. Then the buck stood up and walked by the herd right up to her at 15 yards out. His head went behind a tree and I drew back. Of course he stopped with his chest behind the tree. I held and held until my arm turned to rubber. I had to ease up. Then he stepped out and for whatever reason the two of them touched noses. I drew back again, this time with a wobbly arm. Having invested so much time I had to try. The arrow went way high and caught him just under the skin above his shoulder. He took off and instantly there were deer everywhere around me. I was so deflated I did not even try to shoot a doe.

That was the end of the season and, yes, I ate a lot of beans that year. Looking back at that experience, I might have given it all up and found an easier pastime. But there had been so many rewarding moments that season outsmarting does and smaller bucks that I was sure it was well worth it. The disappointment that day was huge, but I got over it. By the next season, I would be ready, and "it would be easy!"

Wide Rack

Kathy with the backtracked buck

Chapter 7: The Primrose Path

"The true measure of success is how many times you can bounce back from failure" Stephen Richards

The Primrose in Irish folklore is the first rose to bloom in spring and is often used as a sign of hope for the coming year. But in modern times, the term "Primrose Path" is meant to describe how we think things should go, but in the end are a disappointment because we did not factor in a few important details. It is a fitting description to the following stories.

If up to this time I have made it sound like my hunting experiences have been mostly one giant success story, I apologize. The truth is I've had my share of disappointments in the woods. I suppose there is a point when you can spend too much time with the details of bow hunting. If you want everything perfect you may never get to the woods. But on the other hand, every time I hear the words, "Ah, it will be okay," my jaw tightens and I think about the times when it wasn't okay because I hadn't taken the time for the details.

I have a rack in my shed that I set out to look at every fall to remind me that "It won't be okay unless I make it okay!" It is a tall symmetrical eight point that measures 140+. It came from a buck that walked through a bed broadside at 20 yards totally oblivious to my presence. At that time, I was shooting my first high speed compound, a single cam that I struggled to keep tuned. It took a lot of practice to make that bow shoot accurately. This particular fall I simply did not take the time to practice enough.

He was moving to my left at 25 yards and I stopped him with a quiet meaah. I saw the arrow go left and hit just in front of the shoulder. It was not a good feeling and I was afraid there were not enough vitals there to put him down. The blood trail was surprising and I took it almost 200 yards into a standing corn field. Then things slowed down but I stayed with the trail. Near the far edge of the field, I kicked up a coyote that had also found the trail. The buck went back into the woods traveling in a circle. When he jumped the fence back into the woods, he left a bloody corn stalk hanging on the fence. I suspected that the coyote spooked him and he plowed through the stalks. I pressed on into the woods another 200 yards, but the trail was getting hard to follow. I stopped on a side hill overlooking a creek bottom of heavy brush. I had traveled over 500 yards. There below I caught a glimpse of a large deer moving slowly through the brush another 100 yards away. It was about noon and I had made the shot about 9:30; I decided to hold fast. After an hour I moved ever so slowly to the spot where I had seen the large deer, but found nothing. Not wanting to drive him out of the woods, I snuck away deciding to pick it up the next morning. But the next morning I was needed at a Veterans Day program at school, so I wasn't back in the woods until after 12:00 with serious snow moving in. I searched every foot of the area where I had seen the deer, but to no avail. This is the kind of situation, especially when you get tired that the mind will take you down the wrong path. You add up the evidence: a poor hit, a lost blood trail, an animal moving 2 ½ hours after the shot, and nothing found with several hours of scouting. At dark I left the woods trying to sort it all out. I decided that the next morning with 3 inches of new snow, I would take a stand for a few hours near the place that I last expected him to be. No crows called, no coyotes yipped or were moving. At that point I gave up! I made a slow walk home right through the middle of the woods, but I never checked out the area around the stand from where I made the shot.

I hunted hard the rest of the season but never got another opportunity at anything nice. For the weeks that followed I couldn't shake the feeling that I really didn't deserve another chance anyway. About three days into the gun season that followed, one of the gun hunters who hunts our timber every year drove up to my house. Out of the back of his truck, he pulled the head of that buck. "Does this look familiar, Bob?" "Where did you find it?" I asked. "About 50 yards down from your stand on the point." That was the stand I shot him from! It is hard to describe the feeling that came over me. I was determined to never let that happen again. But how? One thing for sure is I practice shooting every day during the season, even if it is only a few shots. I try never to shoot unless I am confident of a good hit. And that particular bow and I have parted company. But most of all, I try not to let my mind take me down the wrong path! Has it worked?

Well, it almost happened again this year! The story I just shared happened 10 years ago. This year on the exact same day of the year, the day before Veteran's Day, I was doing an evening hunt in a courting yard. From behind me, straight downwind, came a nice 9 point that I didn't see until he was heading up the far hillside 35 yards out. He appeared relaxed and I tried to tell myself that he wasn't big enough. He disappeared over the ridge. A half hour later, a doe came at me with that buck right on her trail. At 75 yards out I guessed him to be too small and didn't pick up my bow. She took him by me at 10 yards when I finally realized that he WASN'T too small! He spotted me trying to pick up my bow but he kept coming. Twenty yards out he turned broadside to stay with the doe. I put the pin tight behind the shoulder and fired. He jumped sideways and flew past the doe, heading up the edge of the ravine. The timber's edge was 150 yards and bordered a CRP field full of big bluestem and tall Indian grass. I watched him close but never saw him leave the woods. Not wanting to lose the trail to darkness I waited only 10 minutes and then got out of my stand. The arrow laid in the brush, not stuck in the ground. My heart sank as I could see almost no blood on the arrow, only a coating of what appeared to be fat. The shot had felt perfect. I started on the blood trail and lost it within 75 yards. I searched the ravine that angled up into very heavy cover away from the CRP field. Nothing.

Darkness settled in and I started to see why I valued the morning hunts so much. Picking up a flashlight at home I headed back out. Try as I might I could not pick up the blood trail. My son, Mat joined me with a brighter spotlight, but to no avail. He headed home, but I stayed out for another hour stumbling around in the heavy cover in the woods. Not having seen him leave the woods, I was convinced he wanted to stay in the prickly ash and gooseberries of the woods. That night, it got down to 16 degrees. The next morning there was no Veterans Day Program because of Covid-19 so I headed to the woods to continue the search. Daylight did not help my tracking. I could not continue the blood trail and didn't want to start looking in the CRP field. First of all, I did not see him go into the field, and second, the grass was over my head! But I was running out of options. There was a fire break mowed around the field next to the timber 40 feet wide. I decided to walk the fire break looking into the woods at my stand 150 yards in to see if I really could have seen him after the shot. About the time I realized that I probably couldn't have seen the buck from my stand, I noticed a heavily used trail coming out of the woods. I took it to the tall grass, and there it was, a blood trail that a child could follow. Mat joined me just then, and in less than 10 minutes he found my buck. Field dressing it we pulled the lungs out with a perfectly centered shot. He had traveled a total of 400 yards. A good track runner could do a 400 in 1 minute. That buck probably did it in less than 20 seconds! He must have slowed down in the tall grass, making the blood trail visible. Oh yes, he scored 139 5/8! I almost had gone down that primrose path again!

I have found that path to have many "intersections" and once you are on it, it becomes difficult to get off. Over the years I've had three opportunities at really big bucks, 170+. Each time they had come within five yards of my tree and in some way my mind would head me down that path. It is hard not to get upset just thinking about it. Once might be understandable, but three times? Opportunities at really big bucks don't come along very often in my hunting area and I suspect it is much the same for most bow hunters.

The first encounter was not long after I got my first compound bow, a 70# Jennings T star. It was big and heavy but reliable. Not completely used to it, I started experimenting with different anchor points and shooting with fingers and no peep sight. I admired my traditional bow hunting friends who made their own bows and arrows. Wanting to be somewhat traditional I tried to keep things simple but effective. Lowering the anchor point made me shoot much higher and I had to raise the sight pins. This meant if I went back to my old anchor, the arrow would go way low. Well, I hadn't shot enough to make the new anchor automatic, and I knew it. But I was sure I'd remember at crunch time and "everything would be okay."

On that fateful morning, from the same bed that I shot wide-rack a few years later, I crawled in at first light just a few minutes late. I looked out into the valley and spotted a massive buck a hundred yards out coming my way, but my bow was still on the ground. I got it up, untied, and got an arrow knocked just as he came under my tree. He stopped, quartering away no more than five yards out! I released and he bounded away snorting clear across the valley. I've never had and never will have a deer snort after being hit. It was completely demoralizing. I had forgotten to change the anchor point! Looking at the ground, I saw the arrow sticking just inside of where he had stood. A traditional shooter could have made that shot 100 times and never missed! It took a long time to get over that. To make sure that never happened again, I practiced so much that I got severe bursitis in my right shoulder. That bow served me for almost 20 years until I dropped it out of a deer stand twenty feet up.

My second encounter with a monster took place just a few years later not far from the first encounter. I was scouting my neighbor's woods late in the afternoon when I came to a pasture sloping north. It was surrounded by woods and I was on the Southeast corner with a light Northwest wind. As I looked out in the pasture, I spotted a doe 200 yards out. She was really interested in something behind her and I suspected it must be a buck. Looking around I decided to climb a big Burr Oak tree at the corner of the pasture rather than take my chances on the ground. There were fence wires nailed to the tree that allowed me to reach the first limb. There wasn't much more to secure me with, so there I was, only 10 feet up. I had to rely on the tree's enormous size to blend in. The doe took forever, but kept coming, looking back a lot at something. Finally, "something" started to appear in the middle of the pasture, just over the hill. At first, I could only see antlers. Pulling out my little scope, my heart was in my throat! It was a giant white racked 10 point! You could tell he was not sure about coming with the wind but he wasn't going to let his lady friend get away.

It was starting to get late and I was afraid the doe would never get to me in time for me to have a chance at her new friend. Finally, she got within 20 yards and decided to enter the woods to my right. This prompted Mr. Big to pick up the pace but he was not going to enter the woods completely with the wind. He must have meant to circle her and get downwind. This meant he had to come to my left, which he did but only five yards out and I'm only ten feet up in the tree. I kept telling myself "Let him pass, let him pass!" But as he was clearing the fence into the woods I started to draw back – too soon! He spotted something he wasn't sure of and immediately got down wind. Why he didn't smell me I will never know but with stiff legs he circled the doe and came near her at what I thought was 20 yards. His head was behind a tree and I drew back. The arrow shaved the bottom of his chest and the hair flew. He jumped out about 10 yards and stopped, then the both of them moved nervously away into the woods.

Thinking I had not chased him out of the country, I found a tree the next morning in a bottleneck at the other end of the pasture. At first light, he came out of the woods alone at 50 yards heading away. I never saw him again, but it was an unforgettable experience, the kind that doesn't come along very often. To blow it was a huge disappointment. Discouraged, I scooped up a handful of hair to show my wife. I should have been more patient and let him pass or been a better judge of distance for the shot.

The last encounter was the very next year in a bed where I had spent the whole day with 14 does and a buck in a previous story. It was the middle of November and no snow or ice, just a lot of very dry leaves. As can happen in mid-November things were pretty quiet, not a single deer all morning. There were many turkeys in this area and I knew several hunters who pursued them with 10 Gauge shotguns. It was approaching 10:00 and I was getting ready to give it up. Suddenly came the sound of something very large approaching. I was in a crotch of a large ash tree facing north, which meant my back and left shoulder were against one of the large tree branches above the crotch. The bed was to my left sloping to the East. Looking past the tree and over my left shoulder I saw nothing. The noise was getting much louder. In my mind I figured no deer could make so much noise, so it must be a turkey hunter. Panic was setting in! I could not get a good look behind me, but I was sure it was coming from that direction because nothing was coming from my left – but I looked left anyway just in time to see the largest deer of my life walking past my tree less than five yards out! The part of the tree to my left had hidden his approach. He was already past when I drew back. The arrow made a loud crack and buried itself in the ground. There was no blood on the arrow but a few drops on the ground. It had been a very steep shot and I was afraid I had angled off of the shoulder blade. Without a blood trail I looked for two days just to be sure. At the end of the second day, I spooked him along with a group of does. He looked none the worse for his encounter. After the gun season, I asked one of the hunters of that timber if they had seen a very large deer with a palmated rack. They said yes, that one of their guys with a 20 Gauge had knocked it down and as they approached it, the buck jumped up and bolted away! I didn't know whether to feel glad or sad.

All three of these experiences happened 25 or more years ago. I've never gotten another opportunity for anything like those specimens since then. But I would like to think that if the occasion presented itself in the years to come, I will do better because of the lessons learned and I won't go down that Primrose path again! And of course, "It will be easy!"

Chapter 8: Habitat

"The Clearest way into the universe is through a forest wilderness." John Muir

Iowa gets a lot of publicity about its deer herd. Granted there are some areas of the state that do routinely produce 170+ bucks nearly every year. But in Northeast Iowa where we live, the 170 and above have become rare. In my own experience and talking to taxidermists, rare would be the proper word. In 50 years, I have had three opportunities at the big boys and ended up blowing them all. Interestingly they have all been within 5 yards of my stand. Two were in beds, one was on an evening hunt. How could I miss? Well, we talked about that in the previous chapter. Just thinking about it raises my blood pressure!

Iowa is corn and bean country and agriculture takes full advantage of it. The grain feeds the herd but it takes many acres to satisfy Ag interest and more must be better! Were it not for the Natural Resource Conservation Service (NRCS), I shudder to think what the countryside would look like. As a farm boy of old I watch what appears to be a struggle between two forces, and the battle goes back and forth depending on which political administration is in power and who drew up the latest farm bill. The intensity of both factions (Agriculture and Conservation) has increased simultaneously and the result I believe is that we are barely holding our own. I say this looking through the eyes of a beekeeper who makes his living off of the wild!

The whitetail continues to offer excitement to those who want to pursue for trophy, meat, or simply to watch and enjoy their beauty. Reading some of the previous chapters you may get the idea that our hills are crawling with deer. This is not quite how it is. As I drive the back roads to take care of my bees, I'm constantly looking at habitat, and honestly, for the most part it does not seem that exceptional. But there was this one story that I have to share that made me look harder at the land we live in. It took place in 2014. It's a story that got the whole community talking and I found myself smack in the middle of it.

It was mid-June when an older retired guy who lived near one of my bee yards called and said I might want to check my bees because he had just seen a black bear and two cubs coming out of the bee yard. Well, bears are not uncommon around here in early summer, but it has always been young males just passing through and rarely do they create a problem. But a female with cubs was something new. I headed to the bees and yes, they had been there but only a few hives were damaged out of the 30 that were located there. I put them back together and hoped that would be the end of it. But as the days went by it was obvious that it was not ending. In fact, it got to the point that each day we were wondering where they had been the night before. Then suddenly the damage each time got much worse. Half the hives in a yard were torn apart and many were dragged off to the woods or cornfield and eaten. I called the DNR. They came with trail cameras and bags for specimens. The cameras didn't work apparently because the thousands of bees flying by overloaded the camera storage capacity. I could tell the DNR wanted to keep this bear event low key so I went along with them until one day a young lady with her three little kids came by for some honey. She lived on a farm in the epicenter of all of the bear activity. As she was leaving, I asked what she was planning for the rest of the day. She said, "We are going berry picking in our woods." At that point I said "Whoa, we need to talk." When she left, I immediately called the DNR and said we needed to tell people what was happening. They did and it was big news. The fact that a female had given birth to cubs in our area made it an even bigger deal. The effect on the local residents was interesting. 70% were going to start packing guns, but 30% pleaded for peaceful coexistence. Newspapers and television stations wanted the story. Farmers were afraid for their livestock. I tried to keep things calm and told many that I was more afraid of a deer tick than a black bear. But on the other hand, I didn't want to get between a mom and her cubs!

When I asked the DNR what I might expect for help from them, I was told they were sorry, but as far as the Iowa legislature at that time was concerned, these bears didn't exist. I was on my own. Their parting words were, "Remember, these bears are not protected in Iowa!" This last part gave many local residents an exciting possibility. I knew of at least a dozen who started going after them. As the weeks went by, I gained a healthy respect for the bears. But almost no one had seen them.

I was filling up at a local gas station with my truck loaded with empty bee boxes when a young man approached me whom I did not recognize. "You must be the bee guy," he said. "Well, I saw your problem the other day. I was fishing along the river and was walking through some willows and surprised him. He went flying through the trees mowing them down as he went. He is a big dude!" I had suspected by the tracks and the increased damage that there was more to the story than just a female with cubs. I thanked him for the story but still didn't know what to do. I had a good friend that I considered a professional bear hunter. He had dogs that he talked about like most people would talk about their children. Every year he would go to northern Minnesota and hunt bears with his beloved dogs, but not to kill the bears, just to watch the dogs work the hunt.

So, when the number of damaged hives approached 200, I gave him a call. "Dale, I'm at my wits end." He answered, "I've been hearing about your problem. What is your plan?" I said, "Well, I know someone who has a tranquillizer gun and I'm thinking if I could get the bear up a tree and zap him, I'd put him in a 55-gallon drum, haul him up north and let my son open the lid. But I need somebody to get him up a tree." "Well," he said. "I hear your pain, but this is what would happen. We would have to go across at least four farms in the process and someone would get upset." I knew he was right. I thanked him anyway. As it turned out the bear would not have fit in a 55-gallon drum.

Summer turned into fall and I spent a large part of my time picking up after them, there were 5 bears in all. I had hoped that the first cold snap would put them into hibernation. By the end of November, the insulating blankets were on all of the hives. Each blanket covered four hives on a pallet with each hive weighing 125# or more. With the pallet, each unit weighed well over 500#. December came with a warm up during the first shotgun season. I got a call from one of my bee landlords saying that the gun hunters wanted me to know that something was wrong in the bee yard. I headed right down because bad weather was coming. At first glance my thoughts were that no bear could do this. I guessed that with the warm weather, some deer hunter got stung and, intentionally or not, had banged into the pallet with his four-wheeler and turned it completely upside down. The blankets were pretty tough and this one was still secured to the hives. But the pallet and the bottoms of the hives were ripped off and the combs of honey, pollen, and bees were pulled from the bottom of the hives. No deer hunter would do this. Then I saw the claw prints on the blanket, my hand would barely cover them.

The weather turned cold and put an end to the destruction that year. I dreaded the coming year figuring the bears would be hungry coming out of hibernation. The first call came in April. The hives were on a side hill overlooking the river, the location would have made a perfect deer bed. The farmer was a veteran hunter with many trips out West for deer and elk. "Bob, you'd better come down here. I've never seen anything like this!" It was a beekeeper's nightmare! Each hive is made up of two boxes to assure the bees have enough food for winter. Usually, these boxes are glued together by the bees so tightly that you need a pry bar to separate them. In this case, each hive was rolled down the hill and individual boxes were scattered everywhere. I had no idea which box went where, so I just paired them up and put them back on the pallets. It was a miracle of nature that in the coming weeks these bees went back to work as though nothing had happened. But I was getting really concerned for my bees and my business. This was only April and the prospects for a peaceful summer did not look good. A sizeable portion of the community wanted the bears protected. We tried electric fences, but our business had grown to the point that we could not fence everything. I thought that with all of the people that were after the bears, it would be over soon, but almost no one ever saw them. Guys would flag me down on the back roads and tell me not to worry, that they were going to take care of my problem. When I would ask how, it was usually bacon grease and marshmallows. I'd just shake my head and ask if that was better than honey, pollen, and bees? One neighbor did get a picture of the young male at the bait in the dark looking at the flashing camera. Apparently, the bear was not happy about the flashing light and tore the camera off the tree and stomped it into the ground. But the chip survived to tell the story. This took place a half mile from my house.

For better or worse, things started going bad for the bears. The young male got hit by a truck. The big male was found dead by a mushroom hunter. The game warden thought it might have been poisoned by someone trying to kill raccoons with fly bait and Coke. I wasn't sure about that. But when a widow lady called me who owned the land near where the bear was found and asked what happened, I told her what the warden had said. She replied, "Oh well I just use antifreeze." The female disappeared that summer but was seen again the following spring with two more cubs but never gave us any trouble.

People continue to ask me about the bears. I tell them that I think we should be thankful that we live in a place that the bears could call home. But then I think their disappearance does not speak well for how we as humans have changed this world.

Black bears, whitetails, honeybees, and many other species can be seen as a barometer of our stewardship of the land. Their success would be our own, but I am careful who I say that to. I don't miss their destructive ways, but I do miss the bears.

At any rate, there must be a little something special about this neck of the woods if bears could try to make a comeback. This past fall, our son, Mat, who is really into bicycle racing, put together a 100-mile race through the Valley of the Bears. Using GPS, he calculated a total climb of 11,000 feet! That means a whole bunch of hills added up to 11,000 feet up, but also 11,000 feet going down. He also laid out a 50 - mile course for the older set. I won my age group but there was no one for second place!

I look much closer now at the land as I drive to the bees wondering if we will ever see bears again. I guess that will be up to us. If we do see the bears that should mean the whitetail is secure.

82

Chapter 9: Beauty is in the Eye

"Those who find beauty in all of nature will find themselves at one with the secrets of life itself" L. Wolfe Gilbert

I know some guys who put a lot of emphasis on the measurement of a buck's rack. There are even computer programs to take the trail cam pictures and put a score on them. Just last year (2019) two guys came to me with the news that their trail cams picked up a nice 10 point that measured 135. They said if we let him pass, he would make a dandy next year. They said you can't miss him because he has two split brow tines. So, about a week later, I'm climbing into a stand for a bed that was my farthest one from home. Not wanting to work up a sweat on the way in I took it slow but arrived after first light. As I started to pull up my bow, I looked up wind into the bed and there he was about 40 yards out smelling something on the ground facing away into the bed. I could not believe he didn't hear me or see me. He was really focused on something and I was able to get my bow up without him noticing. He was a nice-looking buck that did have 10 points and would go close to 135 I thought. From the angle I had, I wasn't sure about the split brow tines. He had a huge body, nice wide rack, but the tines were not all that impressive. Besides he was 40 yards out, and that's pushing it even with a high-speed bow. It was early in the season and I had made up my mind to hold off for something more impressive. The early season muzzleloaders had taken a 170 class ten point off my creek bottom a couple weeks before. Sons and grandsons of the people I bought the woods from gun hunt the land adding to the pressure which is becoming universal. I tried to be happy for them, wondering what the chances were for another buck like that to be roaming around.

The buck this morning wandered off through the woods somehow not knowing that I was there. I hunted hard for two more weeks with lesser bucks coming by, but nothing to make the heart shift gears. Then on the Tuesday before Thanksgiving in a different bed, the same buck came in on a crosswind, head down and nose to the ground at 15 yards. He was taking his time and I was able to get a good look. There were the split brow tines, but there was no length to get excited about. He was fairly wide and did have some mass. Thinking about what my neighbors said about next year, I let him pass. He crossed my path and barely even paused. As he left the bed I questioned my decision. So many times, I have done this only to end up shooting a small deer in the January season after the gun hunters had picked them over. I've asked myself so many times, "Is this a bad thing? Do I need to score big every year?" One thing for sure, passing up deer keeps you in the woods hunting harder. So, the question comes to mind every year: What does it take to feel like the year has been a success? And then no matter what has happened throughout the season, why do I feel an emptiness when the season closes? I've seen it in my wrestlers, especially the ones that train really hard. Even when they rack up an impressive record, when it's over, they seem to have a hard time getting back to normal life. I've seen some guys that get pretty taken up with having to score big and some will push the legal limit to do what it takes to get it done. I think for those who truly love the hunt and enjoy the natural wonders that go along with it, a feeling of genuine sadness comes when the season ends whether they've got a trophy or not. But all good thing must come to an end they say. And if we have something nice to show for it, the memories of the season will be etched a little deeper in our souls.

All these thoughts were jumping around in my head when suddenly this buck was coming back! This time he came right to my tree but out a few yards, nose still to the ground. I got a good look this time and found the mass of the main beams fairly impressive. Not completely sure it was for the best, I drew back and fired at point blank quartering away. The arrow snapped the front leg on the far side. He was down and dead in less than 30 seconds. It is sometimes scary to see what an arrow can do when placed right.

Thanksgiving came with a family get together which included a little Brittany, Copper, a lively little dog that could cover a lot of ground fast. The deer was already in the freezer. Quartering it up in the bee shed, it was the first time I could not carry the rib cage to the house to be cut up. I knew my years had been counting up, but the buck had a huge body. I had put the rack in the barrel shed, and although I had taken the cape to my taxidermist friend not wanting such a huge cape to go to waste, I had no plans to get it mounted. On Sunday as they were getting ready to leave, my son-in-law asked to see the rack from my buck. I told him it wasn't too exciting and I was just going to put it on a fancy board for old time's sake. Unfortunately, the rack was gone and I was sure the little Brittany had run off with it or a coyote had wandered in with the overhead door open. We both looked everywhere, several hundred yards in every direction. My son-in-law felt terrible that his dog might have done something like that, but he couldn't believe Copper really would have. As it turned out he didn't. My wife, Kathy had snuck the rack to the taxidermist for a Christmas present.

After getting over the shock at Christmas, I decided to measure it. I couldn't believe my math, so I did it again. Each time was the same, 149 5/8". It went on the wall alongside my "rush hour" buck that the Athletic Director had talked me into in a previous story. That buck measured 152 5/8, only 3 inches more yet it looked so much bigger. There is a saying in life that goes, "How much is enough?" I believe we should not get caught up in measurements. A buck's shape, width, height, and mass all go toward appearance. If they have what you like, go for it or let them go and hope he survives until next year.

The whitetail is truly a majestic creature whether it be a buck or a doe. Their gracefulness and intensity are about the finest you can find in nature. It is a paradox that we try to kill something we appreciate so much. Yet without the deer harvest they will overpopulate themselves into big trouble. As hunters we are part of the plan for balance. But the older I get, the less I like the killing and the more I like hunting. I think it is part of the "stages of life."

I always enjoy stopping by my taxidermist's shop to see his latest creations hanging on the wall. His work is prize winning and it brings out the beauty and majesty of the whitetail. But as I take in the obvious beauty of his work, I am reminded of when my father finally brought down his first buck with a bow. I volunteered to do a shoulder mount for him, but being one of my first works, it turned out to be anything but prize winning. After looking at it for several years hanging in his den, I asked Dad if I could redo it. "Absolutely not, I like it just the way it is!" Thinking of that response, we could say, "Beauty is truly in the eye of the beholder."

Early morning surprise

Chapter 10: A Moment in Time

"Be humble, but believe in yourself! Have faith in your abilities."
Norman Vincent Peale

In the early 50's there were almost no TVs in our rural community, but it didn't matter. We used our imaginations more and entertained ourselves fairly well. There was a movie theatre in town that was quite popular. Most of the movies, at least the ones we saw, were Westerns. So, I was introduced to the bow and arrow on the big screen. At the age of six I whacked off a piece of Mom's lilac bush and pulled up some of last year's horse weeds, found a twine string, and away I went terrorizing the pigeons in the hay mow! The pigeons were never in real danger but they flew around a lot. As time went on, my equipment improved and things became more serious. The laminated recurve bow with brightly colored cedar arrows and pictures of Fred Bear and Howard Hill on their big game expeditions were more than enough to inspire a young boy to greatness. But bow hunting for the whitetail never really caught on until the early 70's.

In 1972 Olympic archery was started again after a 52-year pause, and by the end of the 70's, archery competition was exploding. In 1981, I bought my first compound bow and jumped headlong into field and indoor league shooting with my dad, Kathy, and soon the kids there with me. This went on for about 10 years until technology made a major change in archery. The new bows were shorter, lighter, and faster. They also required mechanical releases to shoot accurately. I began to drop out of competitions because it was just too difficult to compete with technology. I fought the change until I dropped my old bow out of a tree stand from 20 feet. It was a big change to shoot with a release. I did not even tell my traditional bow hunting friends that I had gone the way of modern technology in a sport where we all revered tradition. But the performance of the new bows was quite impressive. The speed jumped from 180 feet/second to over 320ft/second. But with all this came the temptation to reach out much farther just because the arrow's trajectory was flatter, farther, and faster. Also came the idea that the endless practice needed with the older bows was not needed with the newer ones. All this added up to a new bow hunter whose success rate could be poorer than his predecessor IF he did not incorporate some discipline with his new technology. By this I mean pushing the range past 35 yards or letting up on practice was a recipe for a wounded deer.

The more serious you are about bow hunting the more time you will be investing. The last thing you want to happen is to blow a chance at a good buck just because you didn't take enough time to practice or you reached out farther than you should have. Enough bad things can happen even if you do all of your homework. We don't need to feed the coyotes.

Somewhere around the year 2000, I bought my first high speed bow. That year the herd was still oversized. So, during the last few days of the January season I decided to take a doe so there would be some meat to show for the year. It was an evening hunt with plenty of snow on the ground. Light was getting low and I was surprised that no deer had come by with so many around. I was about to call it done when a large antlerless deer came at me and passed on my back side. I twisted around the tree and stopped it with a quiet "meaahhh." It was 20 yards out and fairly level with me because of the lay of the ground. At my shot, the deer ran into a deep ravine and back up the other side and out of sight. With approaching darkness, I got down and looked for sign. I had not heard the arrow hit but I could not find it. Since it was a level shot, I figured it was somewhere under the snow. I took the trail through the ravine and out the other side. Still, there was not a drop of blood. At this point I stepped onto the path we talked about earlier and told myself that twisting around the tree had put me out of position and caused me to MISS.

That night I lay awake feeling very uneasy about the experience. Why was a large deer traveling alone at dusk? At first light I was back out to that stand looking in the snow. Still no arrow and no blood. I headed out on the trail again. Not far from where I had given up the night before I saw my first drop of blood. My heart sank. Then more blood! Suddenly it was everywhere! I trailed it to a thicket of gooseberries and the whole place was red. The deer laid down and gotten up multiple times with large areas of red all over. As I walked through the blood-soaked cover, I approached a very deep ravine. Suddenly out of the ravine flew a bald eagle. I stared down into the bottom of the ravine and could not believe what I saw. There was a skull, a spine, and the tail with one bit of hair at the tip. The hide, legs, and everything else were gone! I checked the skull and there were the pedicles where the antlers had been!

It was not a good way to end the season. I suppose if I would have had more confidence in my shooting, I would have pressed on after the shot and beat the coyotes to my deer. All this and the other stories I've shared show the importance of becoming a good shot and knowing without a doubt that you ARE a good shot. So, when that "moment in time" comes, you rule out a miss until you've exhausted all other possibilities!

Chapter 11: The Road Less Traveled

*"Two roads diverged in a wood,
and I – I took the one less traveled by.
And it has made all the difference."
Robert Frost*

In his epic poem "The Road Not Taken" Robert Frost talks about the decision to try a road in the woods that had almost no use by travelers. It was meant to show how decisions in life can change our lives in so many ways. It is a fitting writing to contemplate when we consider trying something in a way we are not used to.

In the mid-80's books by Wensel and Rothhaar inspired many new bow hunters to try methods that they used which were obviously successful for them. At that time, I was able to hunt seven large timbers with little or no competition from other hunters. I tried their ways but never had the success that they wrote about. Most of my focus was on the "primary scrape" hunting that Rothhaar talked about. As I look back, I wonder if my lack of success was a matter of timing. Or were the herd dynamics that they experienced quite different from mine at the time? I looked in vain for the migration to the "primary breeding area". In my considerable searching, I found some very impressive scrapes and rubs. Yes, there were opportunities at smaller bucks on these scrapes but never did I get to watch a really nice buck perform his ritual on the scrape. For sure they used them, their tracks were there.

My wife, Kathy, proved to me once that it could be done. I set her up 15 yards downwind of a big scrape about 4:00PM at the end of October in 1984. She was uncomfortable in a tree stand, so I positioned her on the ground with good background cover. I had no sooner left her for my stand 100 yards away, when out of the unpicked cornfield came a huge buck that she said would dwarf anything I had taken. He walked right up to the scrape, put his head down, and started pawing the ground. He spotted her struggling to get her bow back, and stepped across the scrape to check her out. When he realized what she was all about, he wheeled around and bailed out. When I came back to pick her up, the tears came streaming down, it had been a harrowing experience. It made me try all the harder at scrape hunting, but I couldn't connect. It was about that time that bed hunting was becoming quite dependable, so I gave up the scrape method. I almost never see a big scrape in a bed, yet I can tell you where the scrapes are and they are in the same places nearly every year.

As I look back at Kathy's scrape event I wonder about timing. It was evening at the end of October. Because of the intense bee work in October, I usually saved the real hunting for November and sometimes not until the last part of the month. By that time, did the big bucks really need the scrapes? When you think about all the aspects of the rut, no wonder we many times struggle to put it all together, on time, and not a week late as I'm sure I have done so often.

There are so many things in life that demand our attention and time. Few people have the luxury of being able to hunt anytime they want. Just take October hunting for example. Besides our jobs, there are fall sports for kids and grandkids. It is not unusual for October to have an unseasonably warm spell which put the brakes on the rut and amplifies the bug problem. But most of these things we can see coming and if we can build a little flexibility into our schedules, it might pay off. With modern weather forecasting, keeping an eye on the moon and the calendar, and making use of every available morning or evening, the odds are ever increased for success.

At this time, it might be well to define just exactly what success means. For each of us it is different and as we get older it will become more different yet. When I was much younger, it meant dragging a nice buck out of the woods with a hunting partner. But 50 years into it, I'm okay with just seeing a big guy up close even if he outsmarts me. Or for that matter just having a nice three-year-old come into a bed and push out a doe and fawn that were bedded below me for an hour is okay too. Zapping a coyote makes for a good day. Probably one of the greatest successes is to see someone else get a nice deer when they've used your coaching to get it done!

The last few years it has been enjoyable to watch the woods respond to a little tweaking here and there. When we cut out the ash trees to get ahead of the Emerald Ash Borer, wow! The cover exploded in the form of raspberries, blackberries, and gooseberries. Now we are attacking the ironwood and boxelders as well as planting Swamp White Oak, Black Cherry, and Spruce. These are species that the deer won't decimate as much, we hope. If I was hunting someone else's timber, I think I would volunteer to help with such things as it makes a tremendous difference.

I am adding another food plot next year. My two clover patches are great for my bees and the deer in early fall, but this morning with -20 degrees and 18 inches of snow on the ground – the deer need corn! I am thankful for the neighbors' food plots that surround me but I need to do my part. In these conditions, I can watch the deer plow through the snow on their way to and from the corn plots. They like to stop by our spruce planting just because it is there. It is like a sanctuary for them. It is only 200 yards from the house and I have no stand by it. They don't mess with the spruce but I wish they would leave the basswoods alone; the bucks have them shredded!

There is another method of bow hunting that I have tried with some success on smaller deer, and that is still hunting. This can be an enjoyable type of hunting if you have all day, and in a timber where you are not worried about leaving residual scent or interfering with another hunter. It helps if you've been through the woods a time or two. I keep to a crosswind or into the wind, taking advantage of elevation and staying away from beds for the wind of the day. Stay out of thick brush and stop occasionally with a tree to break your silhouette. Trying to stalk a bedded deer is usually a set up for disappointment. You are looking for the daytime wandering deer which happens often near the peak of the rut. It's also a good chance to look for sign. Earlier in the season the deer are not as wild, especially with a lower wind velocity which helps keep them more relaxed. You have to decide with your clothing if you want to move quietly while picking up all the burrs in the woods, or leaving the burrs and battling the noise from stick free hunting gear. Later in the season there are less burrs, but the deer are wilder. I usually wear a soft jacket and try to avoid the burrs. I want to be that "ghost in the wilderness". You have to train your eyes not just for movement but for color and shape. My friend Frank, from another story, was quite successful still hunting for elk in heavy cover. When I asked him what his secret was, he said, "I just look for the wiggling ears." Above all, take your time, stay higher in the morning, and lower in the evening.

Since we are talking about a "different path", there is a story I'd like to tell, about one of the three years that I ever hunted deer with something other than a bow. There were a couple of years in the late 80's that I completely struck out with bow hunting. So, thinking I could guarantee meat in the freezer, I bought a used

Hawkins 50 caliber for late muzzleloader season. I never intended it for trophy hunting, and after three years I decided with a little extra planning I could do just as well with a bow. But there was one year of the three that proved to be a challenge even with a gun. It wasn't that there were too few deer. It was the weather of late December and early January. Every storm that came through had us in its crosshairs. Since the snow storms of my youth, I had never seen so much snow pile up. There were no food plots around here then. The deer had left my home area, but I was pretty sure I knew where they would be. A neighbor a full four miles away had a big patch of cedars on a hillside so steep it was impossible to climb in the winter. The trees went to the base of a hill where a level B-road hugged the river. The county kept the road open during deer season, and this was January 10th, the last day.

I got as close as I dared to the cedars with the truck. I knew that even if I could climb the hill, they would be watching me. So, I opted to circle the trees and come in crosswind. Since the first two years after we moved back from the city, we lived less than a mile from this cedar grove, so I knew every foot of it. But with all the snow, that didn't make it any easier. I sunk up to my knees with every step. It took much longer than I expected, and by the time I got to within 60 yards of the cedars, the sun was setting on the horizon. I leaned my head to the side of a tree that I was using for cover wondering if I dare get any closer. Underneath the limbs of the cedars, I saw deer moving all over! They apparently had been yarded there for days and had paths in all directions. My time was getting short, but I was afraid to get any closer. Always wanting to be as traditional as possible, I was loaded with patch and ball and knew my range was limited. About that time, for whatever reason, a big doe stepped out of the cedars and came right at me. I believe she was probably being pushed out by an obnoxious buck. I let her come to under 50 yards and with open sights put her down in her tracks, as the sun slipped over the horizon.

I didn't do much dragging – she pulled me down the hill. I field dressed her at home and the next morning when I went to dispose of everything, I spotted two little embryos in amongst it all. I've always had a hard time shooting does, and that didn't help. I know it has to be, but I would just as soon leave the doe harvest to someone else.

There is a special group of bow hunters that spend their entire lives on "The Road Less Traveled". These are the "traditional bow hunters" some of whom use homemade recurve and longbows with homemade arrows. I enjoy hearing their stories and listen with admiration knowing they have rejected the lure of high-tech archery, and yet can still be successful. In my early years I tried several recurve bows but could not get the accuracy I felt necessary at 25 yards. But every once in a while, I try going back to the simpler way of using fingers with my high-speed compound. Usually this is when my shoulder is giving me trouble and using fingers seems to allow me a heavier setting on the bow. Well, the last time I tried this with the bow set at 50# because of the shoulder, I set the target at 15 yards. With a large piece of half inch plywood behind the target -just in case, I leaned everything up against some full steel barrels of honey. At the first and last shot came a loud crack with the arrow completely missing the target and going through the plywood. As I worked to get the arrow out of the plywood, I noticed that the shaft seemed sticky. Looking closer I realized the field tipped arrow had gone through the plywood and into the steel barrel of honey. That was the last time I tried my bow without a release. The experience made me realize that a 50# draw weight "will be OK".

Chapter 12: Raising Bow Hunters

"The way you help heal the world is to start with your own family."
Mother Teresa

Sometime in the 60's my father took up bow hunting. When I came home from service, I got to hear tall tales about encounters with whitetails from a herd that was starting to grow. The stories all ended in disappointment but he kept at it. The county conservation service had a field range with 52 targets that was well organized and well kept. In the mid 70's, Kathy and I moved back to Northeast Iowa with our kids and our bees. The years flew by and soon the whole family was competing in the annual bow shoots and having picnics at the range during the summer. Most of the community soon learned of our passion for archery and bow hunting. The kids did fairly well in school and didn't cause much trouble. So, when our oldest son, Ben, was in sixth grade, on the last day of deer season, I went to school at midday and politely asked his teacher if I could take him to the woods to go hunting. With some reluctance she said, "okay."

By 3:30 we were both in the same tree. I told him there was a buck and a doe bedded in some cedars nearby and I was pretty sure they were going to come by us. I asked him if the doe came first, what was he going to do? "I'm going to let her pass, Dad." He had done his bow homework and for a sixth grader, was a pretty good shot. We had spent hours in our basement shooting pennies hanging from a string. I was above him in the tree and could not see out very well. In less than an hour, I saw him position himself and knew the time had come. Just as the DOE came into my view, he drew back and made a perfect shot. My buck from the morning bed hunt lay field dressed on a side hill not far away. We dragged them out together. It was Ben's first deer with his first shot. I think Dad was prouder than Son!

A few years later, much of my hunting time had been spent in an area about six miles from home where I had shot some nice bucks, and this year the sign was there. I'd set up a couple of bed stands for Ben at home that were not so high and in trees that were easy to climb. It was a Saturday and, given the wind, he knew where to go. I was going to my special place where the big bucks were. The stand that I was going to had a very unusual buck come under it three days before. It really caught my attention because it had three main beams coming out one side. The other side was normal. I had judged it to be a two-year -old with a smaller sized body. Today was early November with warm blue bird weather, and I had passed up an almost big enough nine-point.

Ben had been to the woods with me many times. We had practiced shooting out of and climbing into and out of his stands, so I had confidence in him but couldn't help wonder if he was okay. Kathy knew where he was and that he was to come and get her if he hit a deer. There were no cell phones back then and we had only one truck, and I had it! Apparently at about 8:00AM the unusual buck with the four main beams from six miles away walked under Ben's tree and he zapped it! The excited young man ran home to get Mom and his older sister, Anne. The three of them field dressed it and dragged it home. I expected that if Ben got one, they would wait for Dad to get home to retrieve it. But because of the warmer weather, Kathy decided to get it home and cool it down. The biggest challenge was getting it out of the timber and across a 100-acre CRP field. I was more than a little embarrassed that they had it all done by the time I got home! I suppose it offered an opportunity for a bonding experience for Mom and the kids, but I would have liked to have been there.

Our younger son, Mat, was born to us sixteen years after Ben and came into the world half again as big as Ben. In between the two boys was Carol. The kids all shot in bow competitions but Mat was able to take on a heavier bow much earlier than the rest simply because there was more of him. So, at the age of 12, Mat and I set out to the woods in the dark on the first Saturday of November. It was his first bow hunt. I did not have a stand set up for the bed he was hunting that I considered safe enough and the only tree I could find that was strategic was 30 yards below the bed, but on a well-used path. I climbed up and tied off the stand, slid back down and helped him get started. When he was above my shoulders, I got under him and we both shinnied up together. Making sure he was tied in securely, I slid back down and headed to my bed 200 yards away. Because it was his first stand, I decided to come back before 10:00. As I approached him, he signaled that a buck had gone into the bed above him and was still there. I backed away and got upwind of the bed to drive the buck his way. But while I was attempting that maneuver, another year-old-buck came to his tree and he made a good lung shot that left an easy trail.

Having helped both boys get a good start in bow hunting has been some of the most satisfying events of my life. I feel fortunate to have been able to do it at a time when there were not so many distractions in their lives as it seems there are now for young people. Our kids were able to learn and appreciate nature with a connection that is still ongoing.

One more kid story that has to be told and then I will let it be. Springtime for beekeepers is even more frantic than fall. Queens have to be raised and hives divided to replace winter losses. This is done in April and May – right during Turkey season. I tried bow hunting turkey from tree stands and actually did okay, but the time spent could not be justified if we wanted to survive as beekeepers. So, I gave the turkeys a rest and tried to pretend I didn't hear the gobbling every morning in the spring. But as I watched 12- year -old Mat shoot grasshoppers with a BB gun, I realized he was ready. One afternoon I came home from town with his turkey tag and found a few 12 Gauge magnums, six shot. When he got home from school, he made a target and put it 25 yards from a rolled up sleeping bag for an arm rest. I gave him a couple of light loads to practice with and told him the turkey loads would kick just a little more.

Right at dark we snuck out to the edge of the woods that bordered an alfalfa field and positioned the decoy 25 yards from a huge ash tree with gooseberry bushes around it. I had never tried this place before but it seemed like a perfect spot. Next morning, we got to the woods in the dark and I got him comfortable, but the place was not big enough for the both of us. I found a blown down tree with a big hole where the roots had come out of the ground and nestled in about 15 yards from Mat. His set up was five yards into the woods and the decoy 20 yards into the alfalfa which was six inches high. He had orders to jump up after his first shot and get to the edge of the field in case the turkey got to its feet and tried to get away.

At first light came the first gobble and it was close. I waited until they were really sounding off and about ready to fly down before I touched my homemade cedar box call that an old beekeeper from Mississippi made for me when we used to haul our bees there for the winter. Immediately they answered, and I knew I had their attention. Unable to contain my curiosity, I peeked over the roots of the tree to see if Mat was okay. There was a deer standing right beside him looking at the decoy! The fog was so thick I could barely see into the field. I called once more and got an answer really close. About one minute later K-BOOM. I scrambled out of my hole and there was Mat standing at the edge of the timber pointing into the field. Birds were flying in all directions, but by the decoy was a big ball of something that I feared was the deer! But suddenly there were wings flapping from the ball – quite a few wings! I rushed over to Mat and my confusion resolved itself as I looked at 2 jakes and huge Tom!

These stories must sound like something out of outdoor wonderland, but if I can reproduce the old pictures for this book, you will see that they are authentic. Just reliving them makes me feel blest.

Chapter 13: Hunting Partners

"True friendship is like sound health. The value of it is seldom known until it is lost." Charles Caleb Colton

Love of the out of doors was instilled in me by my father at a very young age. As I grew older the bond between us had much to do with experiences of hunting ducks, geese, pheasants, grouse, quail, and on and on. And though that foundation was laid solid, it was my college years that provided experiences that I never thought possible. Timing is a powerful force, and in this case, my college time was the same as a few other young men who were seasoned hunters and extremely good shots. Together we summoned up enough courage to ask the powers to be at Iowa State University to let us form a Trap and Skeet Club, which they did and we did not disappoint them. My grades took a hit because of spending so much time practicing in an effort to keep up with the others. My two closest friends, Ben and Frank, could run a 100 straight in trap and not even get excited. But their skill in the field was even more inspiring. Frank's dad was a national duck calling champion and passed the skill on to his son.

Ben was my roommate and a mechanical engineer. I was an electrical engineer. He was a year ahead of me and a whiz at calculus. One day, we were coming out of class from the east side of campus, walking west across a wide-open space that the college kept like a park, Central Campus. It was a dark November day and suddenly a gust of wind hit us out of the Northwest. We both stopped, looked up at the sky and then at each other. We ran to our apartment, grabbed our guns and headed to a lake an hour West of ISU, knowing or hoping the sky would be full of mallards riding ahead of the front. This kind of activity did not get us a spot on the dean's list but for sure we never forgot it. We were actually more serious than it appeared about our education. Whenever there was a lull in the ducks flying overhead, Ben would sit in the back of the boat and write out calculus problems for me to solve in the bow while he kept watch for incoming.

All three of us got married while in college and all three wives hunted with us. Looking back, those were probably the most carefree days of our lives. After college, it was elk hunting in

Wyoming and goose hunting in Canada. In most of the exploits I was on the steepest part of the learning curve while the other guys usually knew what was ahead. But when bow hunting came upon us in the 70's, we were in uncharted waters. It became interesting listening to each other's theories and experiences. But regardless of how we approached it, we all agreed that nothing in the field can demand as much time and energy as bow hunting whitetails.

There is another kind of hunting partner whose bond with you can almost transcend life itself. I'm sure many of you have experienced it. It is that between a master and their dog. Kathy and I feel fortunate that we have had 4 such dogs. They each became as one of the family. We lost our last one this past summer. Her name was Belle, a yellow lab whose main purpose in life was to please us. She started out as a timid puppy.

I came home one morning with a turkey over my shoulder, wings sticking out both sides of me and my face all painted up. She took one look at me and ran to the far end of the farm and we had to go get her. Soon, with a little coaching, she grew into a fierce hunter willing to take on anything and had scars on her face to prove it. We had to be gone one weekend, so we left the porch door ajar so she could go in at night or in case of a storm. When we came home, she was parked under the big Ash tree in the front yard with four raccoons afraid to come down to challenge her. That brought her record to 22 that year – that was 22 that never made it to the chicken coop. Her spirit was more than you could ever want from a dog. She spoke to us with her eyes and her body language. Just opening a box of shells would have her jumping off the floor with all four feet at the same time.

Early this past spring I knew something was wrong when she couldn't stay ahead of me when we'd take our walk to the woods. Then she started having trouble getting up and would wobble in the rear. The vet said it was dysplasia and gave us some anti-inflammatory and nerve pills. Soon she couldn't get up at all and would drag herself to the door. For three weeks we carried her outside several times a day to relieve herself and hoping by some miracle that she would get better. Then she got a kidney infection and the antibiotics could not bring her out of it. At first light on her last morning, I carried her out to the orchard and sat down beside her and talked. I talked about some of the special times we had. I told her that I was sorry but even after 40 years of teaching Sunday school I wasn't sure what life would be like on the other side. She looked up at me with her dark eyes as if to say, "what's happening to me, Boss?" Then I gave her one last hug and totally and completely lost it.

I wrapped her in my favorite hunting coat and put her in a grave under the old pear tree and sprinkled it with clover seed, a beekeeper's gesture of hope. In the days that followed I lost my appetite and started losing weight. I could not shake the emptiness. Kathy said we had to get another dog but I did not want to, did not ever want to go through that again. My granddaughter told me not to feel bad, that Belle would always be in our memories. I told her thank you, but when I wake up and see her empty bed I know she is gone, and all the memories can't bring her back. Though it is heartbreaking to lose them, I cannot imagine life without a dog. So, now we have Hannah, another yellow Lab and a ball of fire. But I will never forget Belle. Hannah will never completely replace her, but she has already found a place in our hearts.

At the end of this chapter is a picture of a three-year-old buck under my stand stretching his neck up to smell a branch I had walked under as I climbed into my stand. He walked on through the bed and survived the season. The next March, Hannah was 10 months old and loved to prowl about in our Spruce planting not far from our house. One morning she laid a shed antler at our front door. I thanked her and put it away for safe keeping. Three days later another shed antler lay at our door. Looking closely, I saw it was the mate of the first antler. Looking closer I realized it was from the buck under my tree!

Some of her puppy ways are endearing, but others not so much. Last week I was intent on replacing a wheel bearing on one of the bee trucks when I realized that the squawking I had been listening to for the last 15 minutes was that of a chicken in distress. Thinking a raccoon or a coyote had dragged her off, I headed out in that direction which was into the wind. Hoping to get Hannah's attention to help me, I spotted her on the lawn 60 yards away. I hollered, "Hannah, birds, sic um!" She jumped up and kept jumping as if to say, "Boss, I can't come right now! I have too much to deal with here!" Looking closer I spotted the chicken under Hannah! After a litany of verbal chastisement, I picked up the chicken and brought her back to the coup, none the worse for wear. That night Hannah lay in her usual place next to my bed secure in the notion that she was the apple of my eye! By morning, Hannah had placed two boots by my bed, not a pair, but she had the number right.

Chapter 14: Photographing the Rut

"Landscape photography is the supreme test of the photographer – and often the supreme disappointment." Ansel Adams

In researching the essentials of wildlife photography, I soon learned that any experienced bow hunter has a huge head start on the beginning outdoor camera enthusiast. Yes, we need to learn the basics of photographic equipment, but we will already have learned our subject's habits and are able to put ourselves in close proximity for the perfect "shot". This fact in itself makes bed hunting all the more exciting. The sheer numbers of deer coming into or through the beds at all different hours of the hunting day provides endless opportunity for practicing. My daughter, Carol, talked me into a Sony 6000 which is far more camera than I need, but it takes some really good pictures in a range of light settings that you would not think possible.

After much trial and error, I have tried keeping things simple without compromising quality. Besides telephoto, you have three variables: shutter speed, aperture, and ISO. These three work together to give the right amount of light to the lens while keeping what you want in focus, with no blur on your target. But in the changing light and shadows of the woods, things can get tricky. In the deer stand, it is better if you don't have to keep checking the camera for the right settings as the light changes. But yet auto settings will only take you so far. Besides that, your subject may not want to wait around for you to get everything just right.

At first light I usually set the shutter speed at 1/100 to gather more light. But that is a slow speed and will require a steady hand. Aperture setting will gather more light at a lower f-stop but range of focus is limited. With bed hunting there will usually be trees and brush in the way of the target that will mess up the focus at low f-stop settings. However, the third variable, the ISO will give more light at a higher setting, but setting it too high gives the picture a grainy look. We need to strike a balance that can only come through practice, practice, practice. Sounds like archery.

Depending on the amount of cloud cover, I keep moving the shutter speed up as the time goes by, and then back down on evening hunts. If there are trees and tall shrubs throughout the bed, the f-stop should be at least at 12 or higher. ISO auto should take care of the rest. ISO refers to the sensitivity of the camera's sensor to light. My camera's ISO auto usually keeps the ISO below 1000 using shutter speed and aperture as I do. A professional photographer could do a far better job than my simpler approach, but simple is not all bad in the deer stand. I don't want to be seen!

Good cameras are not cheap, so you will want a good pouch or pocket that is well padded and quickly accessible without interfering with your shooting. Watch out for zippers, you don't want to scratch the lens. I keep a good strap around my neck. My camera has spent a lot of time in the tree stand and nothing bad has happened – yet. It stands the cold better than I do!

Grabbing a photo of a deer walking by is okay, but I really like them to be looking at me. A soft "meahh" usually gives you a pose. This is something you need to practice. I've never had a deer spook doing this, but the camera is always on them when they stop, and I believe the camera helps to shield my face. It's another reason to have a good background.

I began the idea of photographing the rut to prove the validity of beds. There are two pictures at the end of this chapter of the same buck on two different days coming into two different beds. He wasn't hard to keep track of because he had an antler coming out the side of his skull. I have a point ridge bedding area that is in the shape of a horseshoe. It will provide beds for any wind starting from the Southeast clockwise to the Northwest. I have four stands along this ridge 80 yards apart. But, before you give up on this, thinking that this guy is obsessive compulsive, let me tell you how they work. On a day with a Southwest wind, this buck came into the bed for that wind. He spent 15 minutes checking it all over and then left without checking the other beds. The next day, the wind switched to the South, so I moved over to the stand for the South wind. By 8 o'clock that same buck came into the South wind bed, spent 15 minutes then left without checking any of the other beds. This was only a year-old-buck but he already had the bedding phenomenon figured out!

Maybe it is because the years are creeping up on me, but spending so many days in the woods each year tends to make the experiences with the deer turn to mush, I can't keep them in order. Having the camera helps me sort the seasons out. My neighbors like to watch my slide show after each season to see if they recognize any of the deer that they saw or were on their trail cams. It provides an opportunity to relive the year.

Some of my friends ask why I use such a complicated camera when I could do nearly as well with a cell phone. Actually, I have seen some really nice pictures taken with iPhones of the deer in the woods. They talked me into trying my cell phone, which I would be carrying anyway. The end result was not nearly as smooth – I felt too awkward. Younger hunters are much more familiar with the added features of the cell phone. So, before you invest a lot of money in something you are not familiar with, maybe it would be wise to try your phone first.

Regardless of the direction you go, taking pictures of your experiences gives you a chance to look back in time and say, "I did this! Yes, I was there!" Seeing pictures of your encounters with nature can be a powerful motivation to keep going no matter how many years have snuck up on you. This past season I asked many of my hunting friends "How was your time in the woods?" Far too often, their response would be "I just didn't make it out." We must not excuse ourselves lightly. We need to just KEEP GOING! It helps keep our souls healthy.

Chapter 15: The Ratio

*"Look deep into nature, and then
you will understand everything better"
Albert Einstein*

Of all the factors affecting the rutting activity of the whitetail, at or near the top of the list is the ratio of bucks to does. Certainly weather, food supply, cover, hunting pressure, and moon phase all play an important role in the dynamics of the rut. But for the serious trophy hunter, the buck to doe ratio is critical! And yet most hunters don't think about it much, partially because they think they can't change it anyway. But really, all deer hunters are part of what makes it what it is. I have been as guilty as anyone for not harvesting more does. This year I shot my first doe in fifteen years, and mostly because it had ravaged our garden all summer. The gun hunters in my area have done a good job on does for the last two years taking nearly 30 each year, and that was just one group of hunters. So, I tend to leave that job to them. But that is not as it should be, we all need to do our part. Does having twins and triplets steepen an already exponential population curve. With the advent of CWD in our area, hunters will most likely get more serious about the doe harvest. Though the herd population is well below that of the 90's, it has been creeping back up.

It is hard to put an exact figure on what the buck to doe ratio should be to get the old bucks to do more roaming. Much research on doe movement during the rut suggests that does tend to move out of their home area in search of a mate. This tends to support a theory presented by Roger Rothhaar about a migration to breeding areas during the peak of the rut, which I spent countless hours in search of at a time when a bow hunter could hunt most anywhere. Never did I find one of those places for sure, but maybe I was expecting too much activity in a much smaller space than the "breeding area" comprised.

But for sure, if a mature buck had the ladies come to him throughout the rut, why should he stick his neck out and go wandering beyond his home territory? This question has severe implications to any bow hunter expecting to have trophy bucks wandering through his hunting area throughout the season!

Our DNR spends a sizeable portion of its budget trying to keep a handle on the dynamics of the Iowa deer herd. Besides managing the size of the herd for health reasons and depredation, maintaining the proper buck to doe ratio makes for exciting hunting and sells more licenses. As the years have gone by, whether it is from shrinking habitat or land leasing, hunters find themselves hunting smaller and smaller areas. If a trophy buck can be content to stay in his home range, the average bow hunter is going to have a hard time connecting with the old bucks. If the doe population continues to rise, we will all need to step it up!

Two years ago, the DNR implemented a late January antlerless season for our area which allowed a hunter to purchase three antlerless tags just for that season. This was in addition to the other tags they may have already purchased for other seasons. If the hunter filled all three tags and had the deer checked for CWD, they would be allowed to purchase an extra buck tag the next year. It was called an "incentive season". This definitely changed the "ratio" of bucks to does and the effect was impressive. With camera in hand, I was able to bring home proof of what was happening. Though many were repeats, I had over 50 bucks come into beds at 30 yards or less.

But the number of does was less! The bucks were forced to wander to breed. The local hunters like to check out my slide show to see if they recognize any bucks that may have come by their trail cams or that they saw while hunting the past season. But still my quest to get a picture of that heart stopping buck for a cover photo for this book failed again.

Though the past winter of 23-24 was mostly mild, there was a week in early January that should have brought every deer in the area to the food plots and past the trail cams on their way. We had back-to-back storms that totaled 20 inches of snow with wind and sub-zero temperatures during the month of January. But for the most part, nothing extraordinary showed up! This had everyone scratching their heads. Surely if most of the three-year-olds that everyone saw made it to spring, you would think the next season would be memorable. But the truth is, we've seen good numbers of 3 ½'s most every year, and the next season we wonder where they went.   Some of the questions that come to mind are:

#1. Are the older deer more susceptible to CWD or EHD?

#2. Are they more susceptible to starvation?

#3. Are they more susceptible to poaching?

#4. Are they less likely to take part in the rut?

Of these four questions for fewer sightings of older deer, EHD coupled with the extreme weather conditions that promote it, could conceivably create this phenomenon. Weather comes in cycles. If roughly every four years there are conditions that favor the presence of EHD, it would be more difficult for a whitetail to live to the age of 5, 6, or 7. It would appear then that the solution to this problem would be the adaptability of the whitetail, such as a developed immunity to the disease or a developed habit of staying away from stagnant water holes and the midges that carry the disease. However, this could take many years. In the meantime, let us hope for more stable weather conditions that don't promote EHD.

I believe there is another reason for less sightings of older bucks. The 4 ½ year old buck has come to the time in his life when he has learned what is safe and what is not. He has discovered that moving around a lot is dangerous, especially in the company of younger deer.

Finding a food source near heavy cover and away from other deer leads to a longer life. This would explain how they avoid most trail cameras, as most cameras are set where deer congregate. This theory suggests that the old bucks exist, but also that hunting them would take us to a whole new level! When I get that figured out, I'll write another book!

Chapter 16: The Future

"The future belongs to those who believe in the beauty of their dreams."
Eleanor Roosevelt

This is the final chapter of the only book I have ever written. If you have stayed with it this far you must be either curious or a person of hope. As you can tell by some of the stories you have read here, my family and I are pretty close to the land, and the creatures we share it with. We are ever hopeful that the direction our world is going will be positive for all of nature. I have spent a lot of time trying to close out this book with accurate yet hopeful information. The crystal ball we look into the future with can become cloudy when so many conflicting theories come at us, and it becomes difficult to sort out. Most of the people I've interviewed on "The Future" of hunting whitetails all agree on one thing. We need to keep hunting! How we manage the herd with our human interventions is not always agreed upon by the DNR, hunters, insurance companies, or farmers. We all come from a different starting point. Just a simple question of the need for food plots creates some strong controversy. DNR folks mostly say with regards to CWD that food plots are detrimental to disease control. Older people like me tend to remember the winters like 1959 when schools were shut down for two weeks. That winter devastated the deer herd. Intervention by the DNR with bucks only licenses brought the numbers back.

However, in the 2000-2001 winter with snow and temps at least as brutal as in the 1959-1960 winter, the Iowa deer harvest was a record 140,000 that next fall. Increased production by agriculture and holding the line on habitat by the NRCS, two seemingly opposite entities, has made a difference for the whitetail.   In winters like those, food plots would save many deer and provide healthier immune systems.

Although food and cover can enhance the herd remarkably, other forces are coming upon us that are not so easily managed, and puts the future in question. Perhaps to get a clearer look at the future we would do well to look at our past. The first Iowa deer season was not open until 1953 which produced a harvest of 4,000 deer out of a population of 15,000. Fifty years later, Iowa hunters harvested 145,000 deer! How could this be? There are so many factors but probably the most important would be the adaptability of the whitetail. An example of this in our area is how the Conservation Reserve Program (CRP) changed the way deer adapt to hunting pressure. When things get too "hot" in the woods, the deer move into the CRP where the tall native grasses provide near perfect cover. This kind of situation can be very challenging for a bow hunter, so one must keep in mind that it is usually only temporary. Once the pressure eases up, or a good snow pushes the grasses down, they will be back in the woods.

Part of the goal for this chapter was to interview 100 hunters, which at first, I thought might be too many. I was wrong. It has made me realize that there are a lot of deer hunters in this part of the state. The older ones are slowing down, but the younger ones get pretty excited when asked how their last season went and what they think is in store for the future of the sport.

Concern for CWD varies all over the place. I did not talk to a single hunter who has stopped hunting because of it. Most will have their deer tested if the opportunity presents itself. All believe we need to keep hunting. Most all believe there will always be deer to hunt. Some believe the number of trophy deer will be diminished.

Probably highest on the list of concerns, especially for the younger hunters, is will they always have a place to hunt other than public hunting areas? They see large tracts of land being bought up and then leased for hunting rights. It's also a concern for beekeepers because when the land gets sold, the bees usually have to go! I am hoping that this attitude is temporary and soon people will allow their mental pendulum to swing back to center and realize the important part that hunters play in our environment- as well as the honey bees!

DNR statistics are in for the 2024-2025 deer season. Over 100,000 deer were harvested which is a good number but it is down 500 from the previous season. Significant pressure on the deer herd has been felt over the last two years from Epizootic Hemorrhagic Disease (EHD). In the 12 months of 2024, there were 2,700 deer reported dead presumably by the disease which seems more prevalent in dry years. Weather patterns have not been favorable for the whitetail in its fight against EHD for the past 2 years and many sources predict another dry summer coming in 2025.

CWD testing was more positive. Out of 5459 samples, 51 were positive, and 45 suspected. That is actually down from the previous season of 127 total positive samples. However, the number of counties that had positive samples for CWD has inched up to 25 out of 99. Iowa's total number of deer hunting license sales (from bow and firearms) has held strong with over 200,000 sold.

For my part, the anticipation of the next hunting season keeps me motivated to get my work planned and done so that I can enjoy every possible day in the woods. As the years have been flying by, it has become a tradition that on the first morning out, as I top the first hill heading to the woods, I get down on my knees and thank the good Lord that I have made it to another season!

Looking back on my own fifty years of hunting whitetails, I can honestly say that the greatest value of the experiences lies not in the trophies taken or the meat in the freezer. Rather it is the learned appreciation of one of nature's finest creatures and the environment in which it makes its home. It is my hope that all of you will be able to say the same if you are blest with fifty years in the woods.

PRIVATE
PROPERTY
NO TRESPASSING

WARNING
PRIVATE
PROPERTY
NO HUNTING
NO FISHING
NO TRESPASSING

More habitat creates a brighter future for bow hunting.

Postscript
The Story on the Cover

"Adopt the pace of nature: her secret is patience." Ralph Waldo Emerson

At first glance one might ask why someone would use a picture of a tree for the cover of a book on bow hunting. But after a closer look and remembering some of the details present herein, you might say, "I see!" But there is even more than meets the eye when you know what happened here.

There is a part of my woods that I like to leave alone and stay out of for the entire season. It's not a big place and sits kind of by itself. I stay out of it in hopes that the big guys will feel comfortable frequenting it knowing there has been no human incursion. It has a point bed as talked about in "Recognizing the Bed", with plenty of cover mostly in the form of prickly ash and gooseberries. Since we took out the ash trees, the place has become brushier to the point that an old buck might want to call it home. In one of my first chapters that was written four years ago when I first started this book, I talked about staying out of a mature buck's home bed. But now I have to say that there comes a time. This is the story.

The neighbors had told me early in the season that their trail cameras had picked up three nice bucks roaming the area (at night of course), and that passing up the 3 ½ year olds was finally paying off. I continued staying out of this point bed thinking that surely one of them would come through one of my many other beds during the peak of the rut. Well, I'm sure they did, but not when I was there, nor did they come by any of the neighbors' set ups either. I reasoned that these were smart old boys, so the time had come to try something different. On Wednesday before the opening day of the gun season, the wind came around to the southwest at 8-10 mph but was forecast to get wild later in the day to over 30 mph. This bed was meant for a southwest wind.

The temperature was 9 degrees at 6 AM when I started for my stand in the dark. I had put it up a couple of years before but had hardly ever used it. At first light, I looked up the hill to the beds where I was sure they would lay. In disappointment, I thought, "The bed is too far

away. Why did I pick this tree for a stand!"
Looking over the hillside, I realized that my big
Red Oak tree offered the only descent
background cover available, and with the hillside
so steep, they would be looking right at me. I
needed all the background I could get. Telling
myself I would take them coming or going from
the bed, I nestled in pretty well bundled up.

At 8:45 a set of antlers came from the far
side. It was a nice 3 ½ year old and he wasted no
time plopping down right where I expected him
to go, 40 yards away!   Immediately he closed his
eyes. Five minutes later the big buck came in
choosing a spot just above the first one, still 40
yards away. I never saw him close his eyes.
They had been traveling together. As 40 yards is
beyond my confidence range even without the
brush that hid them, I prepared myself mentally
and physically for a long wait. My hope was that
when the wind picked up, they would move down
the hill right under me.

Two hours later they both stood up, turned
around and laid right back down. Then one hour
later the wind starting getting wild. My tree was
swaying back and forth and blew my gillie hat off
to the ground below. Finally, the smaller buck
moved down the hill and bedded 10 yards out. I
kept thinking, "Okay Big Guy, it's your turn."

But he never moved. At 12:45, after 4 hours of watching them, the smaller buck stood up and slowly walked away in the direction they had come. Then Big Boy stood up and watched the other buck leave. He paused just for a minute, and all I could think of was "what a magnificent animal." Not wanting to be left without a body guard, he walked off with the smaller buck.

Not giving up completely, I came back at dark and moved my stand to a big basswood tree just 15 yards below their beds. The tree had absolutely no background to it, so I hauled in a bunch of evergreens and hung them around my stand. The wind was not right the next day, so I waited until the following day, the Friday before gun season. Again, right at 8:45 came the 3 ½ year-old and plopped down in the same place, and within 5 minutes his eyes were closed. And once again after an hour, the wind picked up and he started down the hill, only this time he stopped where I had loped off two prickly ash branches two days before! It was too much for him and he left. His big friend never showed up!

Although a huge disappointment, the picture and the story brought into play most every aspect that bed hunting offers. The place had heavy cover, the steep hill in front, the wind behind them, lack of human activity, a place to get out of high wind. It was picture perfect and it ALMOST worked out!

The picture on the cover is now the screen saver on our computer. Every day as I look at it, I think of next fall and all the lessons to be learned because the learning never stops!

To all of you who have stuck with this writing, I wish you the best of luck. Enjoy the gift of time with nature and please be careful.

The sleeping body guard

Bibliography

Cox, Spencer. (2025) Photography Basics: The Complete Beginner's Guide. Retrieved from http//www.photographylife.com

Iowa Department of Natural Resources (November 21, 2023). DNR Continues to Monitor for Chronic Wasting Disease. Retrieved from http//www.iowadnr.gov

Iowa Department of Natural Resources (July 26, 2024). Help the DNR Track Hemorrhagic Disease. http//www.iowadnr.gov

Larson, Erin, DNR Deer Herd Health Specialist (April 28, 2025).   DNR Releases Summary of CWD Sampling Efforts. Retrieved from http//www.dnr.wisconsin.gov

Rothhaar, Roger (1982). In Pursuit of Trophy Whitetails. Ojai, CA: Blue-J, Inc

Stone, Larry (2003). Whitetails: Treasure, Trophy, or Trouble? Des Moines, Iowa: Iowa Department of Natural Resources

Black Bear Picture, p.91, Istock. Annalise Kaylor

Acknowledgements

This book is dedicated to my wife, Kathy, who has been my partner in the woods, in the bee business, and in life. Her encouragement has kept me going through success and failure, and without whom this book would never have been.

Also, to our children and grandchildren who politely roll their eyes at our struggles with technology, but wholeheartedly embrace the beauties of nature.

And to the memory of my parents who instilled in me the value of faith, hard work, and love for the earth.

About the Author

Robert (Bob) Fassbinder was born in Elkader, Iowa in 1946. He grew up on a small farm in Clayton County which had a large timber and two creeks nearby where he spent much of his free time. After graduating from high school, he enlisted in the Navy and was trained in electronics. After discharge he enrolled at Iowa State University and graduated with a degree in Electrical Engineering. While attending ISU, Robert met and married the love of his life, (Kathy). The two then moved to Des Moines, Iowa. There he worked as an engineer for a power company for three years, all the while learning of his true passion, to be a beekeeper. In the spring of 1976, Bob, Kathy and two children (Anne and Ben) moved back to Northeast Iowa to start their bee business. Bow-hunting had already captured their attention while in college, but moving back to the hills of Northeast Iowa, the sport for them exploded! After spending countless hours in nearby timbers, he has decided to share with others the phenomenon of bed-hunting whitetails, which taps into the science of the deer's world. This is their story.